Robert Grant

Twayne's United States Authors Series

Kenneth Eble, Editor

University of Utah

TUSAS 426

ROBERT GRANT
(1852–1940)
Photograph courtesy of the
American Academy and
Institute of Arts and Letters

Robert Grant

By Frank Bergmann

Utica College of Syracuse University

Twayne Publishers • Boston

Robert Grant

Frank Bergmann

Copyright © 1982 by G. K. Hall & Company
Published by Twayne Publishers
A Division of G. K. Hall & Company
70 Lincoln Street
Boston, Massachusetts 02111

Book Production by Marne B. Sultz

Book Design by Barbara Anderson

Printed on permanent/durable acid-free
paper and bound in The United States
of America

Library of Congress Cataloging in Publication Data

Bergmann, Frank.
  Robert Grant.

  (Twayne's United States authors series ; TUSAS 426)
  Bibliography: p. 162
  Includes index.
  1. Grant, Robert, 1852–1940—Criticism and
interpretation. I. Title. II. Series.
PS1763.B47   818'.409   81–23765
ISBN 0–8057–7360–6   AACR2

To Sander,
Jill, my father,
and the memory of my mother

Contents

About the Author

Frank Bergmann was born in Germany in 1941 and graduated from German schools. He did graduate work in English, French, and History at the University of Tübingen but also spent a year at Hamilton College in Clinton, New York, where he studied American History as a Fulbright Scholar, and another year at the University of Arkansas in Fayetteville, where he was an exchange graduate assistant and received the M.A. in Comparative Literature. After teaching German and French for a year at Kansas Wesleyan University, he returned to Tübingen to complete his *Dr. phil.*

He was a *Wissenschaftlicher Assistent* at the Universities of Tübingen and Frankfurt/Main before coming to Utica College of Syracuse University in 1969. He has served as Chairman of Utica College's Division of Humanities and is now Professor of English and German, teaching American literature to 1914, comparative literature, Chaucer, and a variety of service courses including German and Freshman English.

Dr. Bergmann has published a book, *The Worthy Gentleman of Democracy: John William De Forest and the American Dream* (1971), and numerous articles, notes, and reviews on American literature and fantasy literature in *Jahrbuch für Amerikastudien, Bulletin of the New York Public Library, American Literary Realism, Mosaic,* and *Canadian Review of Comparative Literature.* He also wrote a brief monograph on Arthur Miller for *Amerikanische Literatur der Gegenwart* (1973). A member of MLA, ACLA, and the German Association for American Studies, he has been active in the profession by giving lectures and papers here and in Germany, by serving as a curriculum consultant in the Humanities, and by reading manuscripts for *PMLA* and Syracuse University Press.

Preface

From birth to burial, Robert Grant (1852–1940) was a proper Bostonian, progressing in due time westward from Beacon Hill to the Back Bay to Mt. Auburn Cemetery. He liked to think of himself as a forward-looking traditionalist, as "a democrat by intellect but an aristocrat at heart." For the better part of half a century, from about 1880 to 1930, he "wrote for and of my own generation; mainly about the class I knew best, the fairly well to do, their manners and customs." Educated—of course—at Harvard, Grant was a judge by profession, yet his literary output was large: some thirty volumes of novels, essays, short stories, and poetry; an autobiography; and a goodly number of uncollected poems, essays, and memoirs.

Conservative in background but progressive in outlook, Grant attempted in his writings to find a way of combining the aristocratic heritage of the Founding Fathers and the rugged Americanism of Abraham Lincoln with the elements of the emerging post–Civil War democracy. This new democracy was marked by the industrial expansion and political corruption of the Gilded Age and by the waves of what Grant considered to be rather low-class and therefore questionable immigrants from Ireland, the Mediterranean, and Eastern Europe. Thus, Grant's topics range from the manners of the well-to-do to the aspirations of the have-nots. Observing what seemed to him a general decline of standards, he exhorts the leisure class to show responsibility and leadership; he urges the social climber to acquire traditional American manners and principles to balance ambition and drive; he sympathizes with woman's emancipation but cautions against excessive demands and inveighs against sexual libertinage, indiscriminate divorce, and the destruction of the American family.

In all his writings, Grant is the "amiable satirist." Representative of the genteel tradition and the realist movement in literature, he occupies a place in a period of American literature defined by the achievements of William Dean Howells, Henry Adams, Edith Wharton, and Sinclair Lewis. He was not as great a writer as these, but his best work—*Unleavened Bread* (1900) and *The Chippendales* (1909)—is a significant contribution to American literature because of its thematic interest, intellectual honesty, and stylistic fluency. Since Grant wrote of his own generation, he was widely read and recognized in his own day; for the same reason, he is nearly forgotten today when even the great writers of his time are no longer household words. Grant's audience—the well-to-do urban bourgeoisie—has moved to the suburb or exurb; its world of today is only faintly reminiscent of his and its world then. Toward the end of his life, Grant recognized and freely expressed his inability and unwillingness to do more than merely observe and register change; he was too old to keep in step with rapidly changing times which he at bottom distrusted. He could, for his part, justly feel that in the midst of his life—of a life which stretched from the pre–Civil War presidency of Millard Fillmore to the second year of World War II—he had done his best to uphold and promote a high order of life and culture in America.

Despite his sympathetic understanding of humanity and his technical facility as a prose writer, Grant never achieved the great book that does not age. Yet some of his characters are truly memorable, and some of his topics—foremost among them his discussion of the role of woman in society—are timely today. However much some of Grant's books deserve to be read even now, he is today generally remembered only for his role in the Sacco-Vanzetti case, in which he figured in 1927 as a member of Governor Fuller's advisory committee that upheld the death verdicts. In surveying Grant's role in that case, I do not attempt to solve the case or to whitewash or blacken Grant's name; I do suggest that his merits as a writer be recognized independently. To show that such merits exist is the chief purpose of this study. Since Grant's work is little known today and since its quality is uneven, I have decided to present much of it in expository and paraphrastic summaries and to evaluate it in the context of Grant's life, time and place; to make connections between his time and ours; and to discuss in detail his major novels and his place in American literature.

Frank Bergmann

Utica College of Syracuse University

Acknowledgments

All references in this book to letters and other manuscript materials concerning Robert Grant are by permission of the Houghton Library, Harvard University. I wish to thank its librarian, W. H. Bond, for permission to study the Robert Grant papers and to publish excerpts from them.

My friend and colleague Eugene Paul Nassar read various drafts and gave me much time, advice, and encouragement. The late Thomas F. O'Donnell was kind and helpful as he always was. Utica College gave me a summer grant and a small travel grant. The professional and clerical staff of the Utica College Library and the typists did their share of the work. My thanks go to all of these and to all the other good people who helped, including Chancellor Sylvia Bowman, her editorial successors, and the publishers.

Chronology

1852   Robert Grant born 24 January at 62 Mount Vernon Street, Boston, eldest of four children of Patrick Grant and Charlotte Bordman Rice Grant.

1854   Accompanies his parents on a visit to his father's relatives in Italy.

1862   Family moves to 5 Chestnut Street.

1863   Enters the Public Latin School on Bedford Street.

1869   Graduates from the Public Latin School and enters Harvard College. Contributor to and editor of the *Harvard Advocate.*

1873   Graduates from Harvard College (A.B.). Postgraduation trip to England and France; returns early because of poor health. Family moves to 14 Commonwealth Avenue in the Back Bay. Graduate work in literature at Harvard.

1876   First person to take a Ph.D. in English at Harvard. Continues at the Harvard Law School. Contributor to and editor of the *Harvard Lampoon.*

1879   Graduates from Harvard Law School (LL.B.). Admitted to the Massachusetts Bar. Briefly active as a lawyer in Boston. First separate publication, *The Little Tin Gods-on-wheels; or, Society in Our Modern Athens.*

1880   *The Confessions of a Frivolous Girl: A Story of Fashionable Life,* first novel.

1881   Extended travel in England, France, and Switzerland.

1882   Appointed private secretary to Samuel A. Green, mayor of Boston. Death of Grant's mother.

1883	Marries Amy Gordon Galt, daughter of Sir Alexander Tilloch Galt of Montreal. Lives at 104 Marlborough Street in the Back Bay from 1883 to 1898, at 211 Bay State Road thereafter.
1884	*The King's Men: A Tale of To-morrow,* written in collaboration with three literary friends.
1886	*Face to Face,* first important novel, published anonymously.
1888	Serves as a water commissioner until 1893.
1892	*The Reflections of a Married Man,* first volume of a series of very popular essays.
1893	Becomes a judge of probate and insolvency for Suffolk County.
1895	Elected an overseer of Harvard College. Father dies.
1900	*Unleavened Bread,* first major novel.
1905	*The Orchid.* Begins a long though ultimately unsuccessful campaign for a uniform marriage and divorce law.
1909	*The Chippendales.*
1913	Fellow of the American Academy of Arts and Sciences.
1914	Active in behalf of England and France during World War I.
1915	*The High Priestess.* Elected to the American Academy of Arts and Letters.
1922	Resigns from the bench.
1925	*The Bishop's Granddaughter.*
1926	*Occasional Verses 1873–1923.*
1927	Appointed by Governor Fuller to the Sacco-Vanzetti Advisory Committee, with presidents Lowell of Harvard and Stratton of M.I.T.
1931	*The Dark Horse: A Story of the Younger Chippendales,* last novel.
1934	*Fourscore: An Autobiography.*

1936   Death of Amy Grant.

1937–1940   Extensive travel in Europe and North America.

1940   Robert Grant dies 19 May and is buried in Mt. Auburn Cemetery, Cambridge.

Chapter One
Beacon Hill and Harvard University

Robert Grant was born in Boston on 24 January 1852. Politically, the year 1852 marks the election of Franklin Pierce to the presidency; more importantly, it belongs to the period of strong Northern resistance—most memorable in Boston in the Anthony Burns case of 1854—against the Fugitive Slave Law promulgated as part of the Compromise of 1850. Intellectually, Boston was "the hub of the solar system" or at least liked to think it was.[1] Its Brahmin authors—Holmes, Longfellow, and Lowell—had assumed literary leadership from the first generation of renowned American authors (Washington Irving was still alive but past his prime, and Fenimore Cooper had died in 1851). Nathaniel Hawthorne was at the height of his career; *The Scarlet Letter* of 1850 had been followed by *The House of the Seven Gables* a year later, and his third great New England romance, *The Blithedale Romance,* appeared in 1852. 1852 also was a year in which politics made itself felt in literature: Hawthorne wrote Franklin Pierce's campaign biography, and Harriet Beecher Stowe's antislavery bombshell *Uncle Tom's Cabin* was published in book form in Boston.

If the year of Robert Grant's birth was of great political and literary importance, the place of his birth was of even greater significance for his personal life and his literary career. For Boston, a city of then about 140,000 people in a nation of about twenty-four million, was not only a center of political and literary activity but one of the nation's largest ports, a manufacturing and commercial center of the first order, and a city of great and proud antiquity.[2] Robert Grant was born in Boston's finest neighborhood, on the top of Beacon Hill, at 62 Mount Vernon Street. Extending from the

State House on the east to the Charles River embankment on the west, Mount Vernon Street has been called "that very citadel and center of the Brahmins, as the exclusive Boston folk of a past generation loved to call themselves." Beacon Hill, rising above the Boston Common, is in the same chronicler's wordplay "Boston Preferred," that is, it "stands for the exclusiveness, the permanence, the fixity, of Boston society."[3]

Sixty-two Mount Vernon Street was not very far from the house where Henry Adams had been born in 1838, and although Grant was not an Adams and therefore could not have drawn the parallel between Boston and Jerusalem which opens *The Education of Henry Adams,* he nonetheless was by birth a "Proper Bostonian," that is, one of the people whose ancestry entitles them to high social status, "whose good manners and cultivation give them a distinction rarely seen elsewhere," and whose self-definition is rendered chiefly in moral terms—by what they will do and what they will not do, in short: by their New England conscience.[4]

A Beacon Hill Childhood

True to the maxim that while "Philadelphia asks about a man's parents; Boston wants to know about his grandparents," Robert Grant begins his autobiography *Fourscore* with an account of his lineage.[5] Descended from Clan Allan of the house of Auchernach in Banffshire, Scotland, Grant is proud of his Highland ancestry, tracing its various branches in England, Russia, Italy, and the United States. He takes care to explain that the name Patrick which frequently occurs in his family is a good old Scottish name and not to be misinterpreted as suggesting Irish roots. Robert's paternal grandfather Patrick Grant came to the United States sometime around 1800 and soon settled in Boston where, in marrying a daughter of Jonathan Mason, he allied himself to one of Boston's leading families. Jonathan Mason was a wealthy and influential entrepreneur and politician; he served in Congress as a senator and later as a representative, and he was associated with the famous architect Charles Bulfinch and other leading citizens in developing the choice residential Mount Vernon section on Beacon Hill.

It was at 51 Mount Vernon Street that Robert Grant's father Patrick was born in 1809. Robert records that "through the Masons my father was first cousin to a number of representative Boston families" (21). However, the social rise of the family was checked when the elder Patrick died in a storm in the Bay of Biscay in 1812: the Grant family never had its "merchant prince" and never enjoyed the large wealth necessary for a truly first Boston family.[6] This did not mean that the younger Patrick suffered either materially or socially; his grandfather Mason left Patrick's mother a house on Mount Vernon Street and enough money to live comfortably. Thus, Patrick received the usual education: he attended Harvard, where he was a member of the exclusive Porcellian Club, "took respectable but not high rank in his studies" (21) and graduated in 1828. After spending about a year in Leghorn (Livorno), Italy, in the banking house of his uncle John Grant—an establishment which some time later failed—Patrick Grant returned to Boston as "one of the beaux of his day," bringing "the waltz back with him from Europe" (22).[7] He became a partner in a commission merchants house, but although he "derived a good income from his business, his capital was not large" (102), and late in life, in 1883, he actually failed in business when he overextended himself in a commodity transaction.

Patrick Grant married in 1840, but his wife Elizabeth Bryant died three years later. In 1850, he married for a second time; his second wife Charlotte Bordman Rice added further colonial luster to the family name, for she was descended from Deacon Edmund Rice, who was known as "the Pilgrim" (24) and came to Massachusetts in 1638. Robert was the eldest of four children of this second marriage. His autobiographical recollections give ample proof of his love and respect for his parents and his close relationship with his brothers Henry and Patrick, his sister Flora (who was particularly devoted to him), and his half sister Anna (Patrick's daughter from his first marriage). In 1862, the family moved around the corner to 5 Chestnut Street. Robert associated with the children of other Beacon Hill families and had a happy childhood, enjoying plenty of pranks year round and snowball fights and coasting in the winter. He liked watching political parades and torchlight processions and would have been delighted by the splendor of Christmas Eve on

Beacon Hill, an observance which did not begin until 1893 and which Robert Shackleton describes as "an affair of extraordinary beauty" with such feeling that generous excerpts of his description are inserted here because they convey the special atmosphere of Beacon Hill more vividly than Robert Grant's own less rhapsodic memories:

> The sun sets on a Beacon Hill immaculately swept and garnished. Every window has been washed until it glistens. Every knocker and doorknob has been polished. And at the windows of almost every house are set rows and rows of candles. . . . Shortly after seven o'clock the illumination begins. One by one, window by window, house by house, the lights flare softly up. . . .
>
> With the first lighting, visitors have begun to come; not foreign-born visitors but visitors distinctly American, it is an American observance among these fine old American homes. The people go pacing quietly about on Chestnut Street, Mount Vernon, Pinckney, Cedar and Walnut Streets, and Louisburg Square—and the fine old district is finely aglow, for hundreds of houses are illuminated.
>
> Enchanting glimpses may be had into paneled and pilastered rooms, rich in their white and mahogany; glimpses of decorous and beautiful living; glimpses of chairs of stately strength, of sideboards of delectable curves, of family portraits by Stuart or Copley. . . .
>
> And at length comes the distant sound of music. . . . When the carolers pause in front of a house a few people are likely to come and stand at the windows; but, if any, it is only a few; no welcoming is expected, no greeting or thanks. . . .
>
> The night's candles are almost burned out. . . . And now, house by house, window by window, candle by candle, the lights are extinguished and the streets go gradually to darkness. Almost suddenly, now, they are deserted. Almost suddenly the last of the people have gone. The houses are dark, whole streets are dark. The entire hill is in darkness. The hill is in silence.[8]

Beacon Hill's special charm is so great that it imbues even rather recently written memories: in 1967, the daughter of Bishop Lawrence—himself a leading Brahmin and a friend of Robert Grant's—called her book *To Be Young Was Very Heaven*.[9]

Robert was a sensitive, impressionable boy. The Civil War reports and the assassination of Lincoln strongly affected him. So did visits to the theater, and early reading which ranged from Mayne Reid and Beadle's dime novels to Cooper, Scott, and Dickens. Other formative influences were Sunday school ("my religious experience, that of a lukewarm yet reverent and sophisticated Christian, began at and is still linked with Arlington Street Church" [44]) and Lorenzo Papanti's dancing school on Tremont Row. He particularly enjoyed the summers the family spent at Nahant, the peninsular resort on Boston's North Shore, where his grandmother Charlotte Rice owned a cottage. In *Fourscore,* Grant recalls with great clarity even minute details of the cottage and its grounds, remembers family visitors and distinguished guests like Longfellow and Agassiz, and relives the excitement of "the most sensational occurrence" (61) of his boyhood, the kidnapping of a cousin who was attending summer school with him at Nahant. A remark on Sunday service at Nahant shows young Robert as a careful and independent observer: "Despite a fairly tolerant point of view of the elder generation—seventy-five per cent more so than that of youth today—I was left completely cold by songs of praise which professed immediate longing for a new Jerusalem. Such a patent hypocrisy could not escape me, it being self-evident that every man and woman in that well-to-do congregation was eager to live as long as possible" (73). More than anything else at Nahant, Robert enjoyed the fishing, swimming, and boating: his lifelong love of sports and the outdoors dates from those happy summers by the seaside.

Grant recorded many childhood impressions in his book *Jack Hall or The School Days of an American Boy* (1887), which will be discussed in chapter 3, but some remarks regarding his school days are in order here. He went to private schools in the immediate neighborhood until 1863, when his father enrolled him in "the Latin Grammar School, or Public Latin School as it was usually called, on Bedford Street, at which boys were prepared for college" (31). The instruction there was of high quality but, as Grant later thought, too dependent on memorization. He did well, frequently received prizes, and graduated with honors in 1869.

A Harvard Education

Harvard College.   For the description of his college days in
Fourscore Robert Grant relied on a lecture he gave in 1896, "Harvard
College in the Seventies," and on an 1897 article "Undergraduate
Life at Harvard" by Edward S. Martin (77). Grant took his entrance
examinations for Harvard in June 1869; these examinations were
in " 'Greek composition, Greek grammar, history and geography,
English into Latin, Latin grammar, plane geometry, arithmetic and
algebra. Besides these written examinations we had to translate
orally Latin and Greek' " (76). He passed without problems and
entered Harvard in the fall of 1869 as a member of "the first freshman
class of President Eliot's long term of illustrious service to education"
(78).

Robert seems to have followed the gentlemanly course of study,
which included generous amounts of social life. He had natural
ability and had received a good preparatory education, so that he
did not need to work very hard to achieve his academic goal, which
was to maintain "a respectable average in the middle of my class"
(77). *Fourscore* gives a detailed account of the kind of social life Grant
participated in. His freshman class was one of the last to undergo
hazing; in his case, hazing meant being tossed in a blanket in the
gymnasium and reciting "Mary had a Little Lamb" in his nightgown
in front of a group of smoking sophomores. He was a lively undergraduate and was several times admonished and once put on
probation for misconduct such as " 'inattention and disorder at Italian exercise' " and creating a racket in his dormitory rooms, located
above a professor's apartment, by "endeavoring to deposit my chum
in the coal closet" (85). He belonged to the exclusive A.D. Club;
the ΔKE, a secret society; and the O.K., a literary society; but he
was also interested in athletics and, though of small size, played
football (which then was much like rugby) and tennis. Consequently,
he was socially well situated and made a number of important
friends.

His immersion in this kind of activity left him with only marginal
interest in his studies and his teachers, although he recalls the
qualities and idiosyncracies of some of his professors in *Fourscore*.

Generally speaking, student-faculty relations in those days were not very close: "Unfortunately a line of cleavage seemed to be drawn whenever the lecture or recitation was over, without ostensible fault on either side" (95). The faculty on the whole was very impressive, but only Henry Adams managed to light a spark in Grant. Adams's method in teaching medieval history led Robert, by now a senior, "for the first time to try to do well continuously in a college elective" (96).

After graduation in 1873, Grant was to spend a year in Europe to see the sights and become fluent in French. He enjoyed the scenery in Ireland and Scotland, did London—where he rubbed elbows with aristocracy—and crossed the channel to settle down with a Parisian family. But the travel had not improved what was at graduation a very slight physique, and on the advice of an American doctor he quickly returned to Boston.

Graduate School.   Because of his immersion in college life, Grant took little note of affairs outside Cambridge during his student years. He was only a curious bystander at the great Boston fire of 1872: "I was too immature to have any part in the work of reha-bilitation" (105), and although he recognized hard times by the old clothes many of the students were wearing, the panic of 1873 made no particular impression on him. His family "had just moved to 14 Commonwealth Avenue on 'the new made land,' as it was still called" (103), following many Beacon Hill residents to the more spacious and newly fashionable Back Bay districts. The new house was given to Grant's mother by his grandmother who had come into an inheritance. "Unusually ignorant of the meaning of dollars and cents" (102), Robert decided to continue his education and indeed received the support of his parents. In *Fourscore,* he describes his situation after his return from France: "The three years immediately following proved to be the most formative of my life. My project to learn French and German having been frustrated, I looked about, dispirited though I was, for the most promising substitute" (102). Having no particular aptitude for or interest in a profession, he entered the Harvard Graduate Department in the fall of 1873 to study for the newly instituted Ph.D. in literature. A loosely pre-scribed course of study included most of the works (in the original) of Chaucer, Milton, and Shakespeare; Lessing, Schiller, and Goethe; Dante and Petrarch. Although free to seek academic advice, Grant was essentially on his own. Though somewhat awed by the ambitious program, he was enthusiastic about this method of study and worked systematically. He wrote a brief thesis and, at the end of three years, was examined by the illustrious triumvirate of Francis J. Child in English, Frederick H. Hedge in German, and James Russell Lowell in Italian. His "thesis, 'The Sonnets of Shakespeare (the various theories that have been given to account for them),' advanced no new theory, and was limited to a discussion of five separate points of view already in print" (107). He passed his examinations in English and German but was nervous going into the Italian test because of his perfunctory preparation of Dante's *Paradiso*. Hoping to be examined in the *Inferno* or *Purgatorio,* he nevertheless was circumspect enough to prepare "on the evening before the examination the last canto of the *Paradiso* with scrupulous care" (106). True enough, the next day Lowell "waved me to a seat and a moment later said with thin-lipped preciseness, 'You will open your Dante, Mr. Grant, at the last canto of the *Paradiso*' " (107). Thus, in 1876, Robert Grant was awarded Harvard's first Ph.D. in English.

Law School. The reading list for the Ph.D., being confined to the great classics of European literature since Dante, does not indicate the full range of Grant's reading during his years at Harvard. Already familiar with the works of Scott and Dickens, Grant now discovered Thackeray and a little later Balzac. His high opinion of Thackeray never changed; he writes in *Fourscore* that "if asked today to name the greatest novel ever written, I should still specify *Vanity Fair*" (108). He read a great deal of poetry as well, his favorite writers being Byron, Tennyson, Swinburne, and Clough. He particularly liked the London *vers de société* by Calverley, Locker, and Dobson—writers of only historical interest today but of importance then for their "polite yet sparkling literature of which American letters was almost entirely barren" (109).

Much as he enjoyed the years of formal study and informal reading from 1873 to 1876, he came to realize that "I could not go on forever without earning money and without a definite calling. I had only reached the point, however, where I was uncertain whether I wished to be a man of letters, a journalist, or a lawyer. Reaction from a glut of knowledge that led directly to nothing led me to fit myself for a profession as the saner course. Perhaps eventually one could be a little of all three" (111–12). To today's liberal arts graduates and unemployed English Ph.D.'s, Grant's problem sounds most familiar.

He entered Harvard Law School in 1876, expecting to graduate after two years, but while he was there the program was expanded to three years. Just as there had begun to be a change in teaching methods at the college and the graduate department, so there was a change in methods in the law school "from the lecture to the case system instituted by Dean Langdell" (112). Some of Grant's courses were torts and contracts, common law, real property, and criminal law. He was serious about his studies: "I was a diligent student, interested in my work and amenable to my instructors" (112). As a result, he "was elected to the Pow-Wow Law Club—deemed to be a compliment—and argued cases before its high court, of which in rotation I became a member" (113). He passed his examinations and received the degree of LL.B. in 1879, was admitted to the Massachusetts bar the same summer, briefly was an apprentice in a commercial law firm in Boston, and soon thereafter formed the partnership of Grant and Peters with a fellow Harvard graduate. All in all, Robert Grant had spent ten years at Harvard, "a record which I doubt has been surpassed or equalled by any other registered student" (83).

Chapter Two

Early Novels of Manners and Fashionable Society (1878–91)

Robert Grant's first literary efforts happened quite by accident. Having to translate some Latin verse into English prose at the Latin School, he mechanically started every line with a capital letter because the Latin text did so too; to his astonishment, he found himself openly commended for "a creditable attempt at blank verse": "No one could have been more amazed than I or more quick to disclaim poetical intent. But my mistake when owned led me to ask myself, 'Why shouldn't I try?' And try I did in the various exercises of the same kind that followed."[1] Soon an original poem called "The Ocean" received a school prize "in spite of the stipulation in the catalogue, 'No exercise will be rewarded because it is the only one presented' " (69).

Collegiate Writings

Grant received further encouragement during his early years at Harvard when his instructor in essay writing commended his prose style in an assignment which required the condensation of a Shakespeare play into four pages. Soon thereafter, Grant began sending contributions to the *Harvard Advocate,* then the college's only paper. He wrote brief poems, skits, and articles which frequently satirized college affairs, and he soon became one of the paper's editors. He modeled his poems after the current London *vers de société,* a kind of poetry he preferred because its "witty, finished lightness suited my youthful mood and taste" (109). His classmates seemed to like his work, for they chose him poet of the class of 1873. He turned to Professor Francis J. Child for advice and encouragement and produced a poem which pleased Child and the Class Day audience. At the beginning of his second year in the graduate program, Grant sought more fundamental advice from the eminent poet Henry Wadsworth Longfellow, who was living in Cambridge:

I have a strong taste for a literary life and in particular for imaginative writing novel writing versifying etc. [*sic*]. . . . Accordingly as I have no taste for law or business or for any other profession, I must choose some branch of belles-lettres to devote myself to, so as to know something well. Would you be kind enough to tell me where you think the best field lies for a student of modern literature?

He also asked Longfellow whether he should study Italian literature and history at Göttingen—Americans' favorite German university—or in Italy.[2] He actually did neither, completing his Ph.D. in residence instead. Nor did his attitude toward law prevent him from entering the Law School in 1876.

About the time of his writing to Longfellow, Grant became "assistant editor of *Old and New,* a monthly magazine with a blue cover, the editor-in-chief of which was Dr. Edward Everett Hale" (107). Three rather labored poems of Grant's were accepted for publication by the magazine, and in *Fourscore* he fondly recalls having received "thirty dollars in compensation for one or another of these pieces of lively, learned doggerel, the first money I ever earned" (108).

While in law school, Grant continued to write satirical verse and prose. These efforts were published in the *Harvard Lampoon,* of which he was one of the editors. Many of his pieces from that early period are undistinguished, occasional, and imitative, but some show wit, a facility with style, and a developing interest in the study of manners—three qualities that became important elements in his subsequent work.

Perhaps the best examples of the *Lampoon* period are the two playlets *The Little Tin Gods-on-wheels* and *Oxygen!* (1878).[3] "A Trilogy After the Manner of the Greek," the first of these consists of "The Wallflowers," "The Little Tin Gods-on-wheels," and "The Chaperons" and is set in Boston, "the Modern Athens." The ex-

citement and boredom of balls is presented from the points of view
of pretty and plain, shy and lordly participants as well as match-
makers and fashion gossips. Complete with marching Greek choruses, the three tragedies sport an assortment of meters ranging from
Elizabethan blank verse to recondite dactylic tetrameter. *Oxygen!*
moves out of the ballroom to the fashionable Maine summer resort
of Bar Harbor. Limited to two characters—Miss Alice Bunting of
Philadelphia and Mr. Arthur Flannelshirt of Boston—it is equally
a spoof of the received methods of courting, but without the pseu-
doclassical garb of *The Little Tin Gods-on-wheels. Oxygen!* ends on
a note of common sense; when the seasoned Alice refuses to entrap
her admirer, Arthur gives voice to his gratitude for such unexpected
magnanimity in the pensive line: "Good-night, good-night! O, why
ain't more girls like her!" (41).

The Confessions of a Frivolous Girl

The *Harvard Lampoon* playlets were so popular that Grant published them in volume form in 1879, at first anonymously but in
a subsequent printing under his name. They continued to find
readers, and it was their success—combined with much leisure time
in his fledgling law partnership—which encouraged him to write
and publish his "first serious attempt in prose," *The Confessions of
a Frivolous Girl: A Story of Fashionable Life* (1880). The commercial
and critical success of this first novel was so great that it not only
established Grant as a writer in his own and the reading public's
view but also pushed him into a line of work which, though congenial and profitable, made it difficult for him later on to shake the
label of pleasant entertainer.[4]

Alice Palmer, the novel's heroine, actually is not at all a frivolous
girl with something to confess; rather, she does not always conform
to the expectations of her fashionable walk of life. It is true that she
does all the socially right things expected of a rich girl in a metropolitan ambience: "come out," go to private school, study literature and history in the off-season, and even dabble in charity, but
Alice is honest enough to say that she enjoys New York and Newport
for the fun of it.[5] She is not interested in catching a suitable husband
and refuses to think of society life as a big chaperoned marriage

market. Rich in her own right, she can afford to be romantic; if she ever marries, she will do so for love, not money. However, she is not ready for either love or marriage; this becomes clear by her repeated cogitations on the passion of love as she thinks it is supposed to be and by her refusal of two suitors. She rejects Murray Hill and Manhattan Blake because she does not want to be tied down for life to either of these men, even though they are agreeable companions when she meets them in society.

Alice surveys the options a girl and a married woman have and decides that they are not inviting. A man always has his work, but a woman turns into a spinster or a doll. If Alice and she do not get married, her best friend Grace Irving suggests, they can live together, with a parrot and two cats apiece. To Alice, such a future is as unattractive as being a man's ornament—especially a socially shelved one, if the husband is not rich. Of course Alice is expected to make a fine, perhaps even brilliant match, since she is of excellent family and such a success in society. But the more confused she is, the less help she gets: her mother has little patience with her individualistic notions. The longer Alice holds out, the greater the pressure on her becomes. Indeed, the jilted suitors—and society in their behalf—imply that she is a frivolous girl, not because she might be a swinger or a flirt but because she insists on her own way.

Finally, Alice marries Murray Hill after all, instead of the wealthy Gerald Pumystone or someone else from among her suitors, but not because of a radical change in outlook. Rather, her aunt has died, and Alice has to be in mourning, during which Hill's steady and quiet attention and devotion change her feelings of friendship and sisterly regard to love. Once married, she adores her husband and their little girl and begins to see married life in a brighter light. Yet all this change happens without fanfare and rousing passion. Instead, there is a great deal of reflection and finally a realistic though not consciously rational choice and above all a lingering touch of sadness at having to grow up.

Technically, Grant functions as editor of Alice Palmer's diary, so that the point of view is that of the heroine throughout. The result is a very intimate, chatty, self-reflective, and self-revealing

account of a girl talking to "dear diary" (which on occasion is allowed
to speak for itself). In selecting this point of view, Grant on the one
hand activates well-known virtuous and romantic literary associations and on the other manipulates the reader's expectations between
compassionate interest and sheer curiosity, particularly because of
the adjectives in the title.[6] Together with "confessions" and "fashionable," "frivolous" gives the title a sensational ring the book itself
does not have. What looks like a sensational or at best ambivalent
title before the reading afterward appears as ironic, and the distance
between initial expectation and final evaluation constitutes the
growth in the reader's critical perception of manners. Though a
pleasant book, *Confessions* is primarily a serious one; it surely does
more than break "social butterflies upon the wheels of satire."[7]

The Confessions of a Frivolous Girl is not a deeply searching novel,
but it is an honest view of the problems of a girl who should not
have any. In its discussion of the friction between feminine individualism and societal codes it announces Grant's later novels,
though with greater sympathy for the heroine; unlike so many of
her successors, Alice Palmer is thoroughly likeable. Without being
overly imitative, Grant's delicate to heavy satire is indebted to Henry
James, and his ridiculing of the American tendency to lionize foreign
dignitaries—his cast includes the Honorable Hare Hare, future earl
of Hammerhead, and Muchfeedi Pasha—moves the book close to
the contemporaneous political satire of John William De Forest and
Henry Adams.[8]

Confessions was well received, and for a brief moment Robert Grant
considered taking up writing as a livelihood: out of his association
with the *Harvard Lampoon* came an offer, in 1883, to move to New
York and become an owner and editor of *Life*. Grant was reluctant
to leave Boston, "but the controlling objection was my sudden
realization that the necessity of being humorous once a week for
fifty-two weeks in every year, without much leisure for anything
else, would result in a nervous breakdown." It was a wise realization.
Unsure of his talent, Grant did not want to see its potential destroyed
by hack writing. His career lay elsewhere: as he had hoped in 1876,
perhaps he could eventually be lawyer and journalist and man of
letters all three at the same time.[9]

Success as a lawyer, however, was slow in coming. The firm of Grant and Peters was of no long duration, as Peters soon withdrew for personal reasons. The firm's most memorable case seems to have been a wage claim in behalf of a number of sailors; the claim was adjusted, but the partners' ignorance concerning negotiable instruments made them endorse a worthless draft the sailors presented, so that Grant and Peters not only rendered services for nothing but lost money in addition.

Since business was slow, Grant had leisure to enjoy social and outdoor life. He fondly recalls balls, parties, and ice-skating dates, all of which brought him together with young men and women of his own class. Even though "the American girl was a goddess for whom nothing was too good and with whom no liberties could be taken" (128), Robert "knew a score of girls so well that we discussed everything except the processes by which children are brought into the world" (127). As early as 1875, he was invited by various personal and family acquaintances to go salmon fishing in the province of Quebec, a sport which he kept up almost to the end of his life. In 1881, he once again traveled in Europe, though with no design to revive the study of languages he had had to abandon in 1873. He visited London and Paris and enjoyed the beach at Étretat, but the high point of his travels came when he climbed a mountain near Zermatt in the Swiss Alps and saw, in the early morning light and in the glory of freshly fallen snow, the "marvelous panorama of Monte Rosa, the Matterhorn, Breithorn, Lyskamm, and a host of other peaks and glaciers" (154).

Back in Boston, he was chosen a member of the Papyrus Club, an assembly of witty bohemians of talent and means. Grant records: "It was due to one of this group, George F. Babbitt, a capable journalist and my good friend all his days, that I became in 1882 the private secretary to Samuel A. Green, the recently elected Mayor of Boston" (125). Green wanted "a young man who is a gentleman and a graduate of Harvard" (157); Grant was recommended and appointed at a salary of $3,500, considerably more than he was making as a lawyer.

An Average Man

Grant was pleased by the success of *The Confessions of a Frivolous Girl,* but there remained in his mind the doubt whether he could write a really serious-minded, dignified book. When he was approached in 1882 by James R. Osgood, a publisher who "was on the lookout for promising young writers," he attempted to write such a book with *An Average Man* (1883), but he was conscious of writing against his grain and therefore severely critical of the result. [10]

Arthur Remington and Woodbury Stoughton are Harvard classmates; after some foreign travel, they continue on together through Harvard Law School. After graduation they set up law practices in New York City, a place which in its own set of contrasts underlines the differences between the two friends. Woodbury is handsome, self-assured, quite the gentleman, well read but rather practical and pragmatic, bent on money and success. At Harvard, he is "tacitly pigeon-holed as an embryo Chesterfield" (21). Arthur is handsome also but of less commanding presence, more ethereal and more idealistic. New York teaches them the reality of life from which the university had largely shielded them. It is a fast-paced city: "All was glitter and roar and rush and hurry. The universal movement was of a race where each one fears to be left behind" (1). It is a town of sharp contrasts, "where Virtue and Vice touched each other's cheek,—where Plenty delights to flaunt, and Want to sun itself" (1). It is a place which "knocks the romance out of one very fast" (5), and where money rules everything.

The two friends make many acquaintances. Among them are Eugene Finchley, who foreshadows the self-made success of Blaisdell in *The Chippendales* (1909); Mrs. Tom Fielding (Ethel), a charming but unhappily married socialite; some of Ethel's friends, notably Dorothy Crosby; and the Idlewilds. Peter Idlewild is the typical success story which Finchley hopes to repeat; from small New England beginnings he has risen to be a wealthy banker and railroad baron. Grant uses the variegated but essentially upper-class social panorama to discuss many questions about life in general. Mrs. Fielding, giving voice to her personal disappointment, declares that " 'we lack passion as a nation,' " that " 'we are artificial and cold. We are forever repressing ourselves' " (50). The hustle and bustle of the metropolis undermines Arthur Remington's innocent childlike belief in the moral superiority of the United States and the intellectual makeup of his compatriots. The roles of man and woman are thoroughly discussed and presented, but once again only from the limited viewpoint of the upper class. Peter Idlewild has come to conclude "that democracy avails women little, and that their only chance for prominence lies in social prestige" (59). Dorothy Crosby envies in a vague way the opportunities men have, but she clings strongly to her notion of femininity, even though her role in life is not very clear to her. Arthur shares his romantic opinion with her: " 'I believe a truly noble woman is the divinest thing in creation, and that she can raise the man who loves her, and whom she loves, up to those shining stars whose ministrant she is. That is her power; that is her mission' " (173). Slowly—piece by piece—a general picture of life and society emerges, a tenuous compound of social Darwinism, positivism, and Concord idealism, perhaps most clearly expressed in an authorial reflection on Dorothy's character and heritage:

We bear fruit in our descendants, and individual effort is the secret of the progress of the world. A man's possibilities are decided in his mother's womb. Each one of us mortals has his limits,—his gamut, so to speak; and the best performer cannot strike a note to thrill the soul from a low-priced instrument. Life is a growth, and whosoever touches the stops aright will, though he play himself a feeble strain, transmit to his children the power for sweeter melody. (53–54)

Slowly the two friends drift apart. Stoughton dabbles in politics and learns how to mix pragmatism and principle to get ahead. In the process, he loses many of his fine qualities and some of his previously irreproachable reputation. He marries Isabel Idlewild, who is much in love with him, but he—cold puritanical soul—does not respond to her whose intellect is far beneath his but whose emotional warmth could make him whole. Remington advances far more slowly and finally reaches what can best be described as genteel poverty. He proposes to Dorothy Crosby but is rejected; three years later he offers himself again and is accepted. In the meantime things have come to a head for Stoughton. He makes an effort to buy votes but loses the congressional election to Finchley. His marriage has

gone sour, despite a baby and Isabel's continuing love. He and the
disappointed Ethel Fielding find one another. By accident, Isabel
sees them together in Central Park; deeply wounded, she returns
home only to learn that her father is on his deathbed. She files for
divorce; Stoughton sails for Europe and is followed by Ethel who,
however, is very soon left alone at Chillon: Stoughton no longer
loves her and goes to London, presumably looking to make a new
start in business. Isabel spends much time with the happily married
Remingtons and finally becomes their neighbor. Dorothy persuades
her to drop the divorce suit, and the novel ends on a quiet note of
charity: Isabel will learn to be useful to the world through her
wealth.

   Grant alternates tense and action-packed scenes with very leisurely
and descriptive ones. Occasionally, he achieves perfect setting and
mood, accompanying and foreshadowing the action, notably so in
the Central Park episode. Some of the reflective scenes, usually given
from the particular character's point of view, are, however, decidedly
flat, and some of the dialogue is stiffer and more boring than the
characterization of a particular social scene requires. Thematically
too the novel is uneven. Who is the average man? Stoughton or
Remington or Finchley? Neither, really. Certainly the lower classes
are excluded, though indirectly there is a sense of their latent power
in Stoughton's comment that "it was the very ignorance of the
miserable classes and their lack of insight into reality, that were the
protection of society" (268). Stoughton's political career gives Grant
a platform for much pertinent observation and comment on political
matters including the civil service reform so strongly advocated by
Henry Adams, but ultimately Grant does not adequately integrate
the political and sociological material with the novel of manners.
Between peripheral lower-class figures and machine politicians, self-
made men and wealthy as well as comparatively poor aristocrats, no
discernible portrait of an average man emerges.[11]

   While Grant was working for Dr. Green and writing for Osgood,
his personal life saw major changes. Early in 1882, his mother died.
Although she had not been well for some time, her sudden death
came as a surprise. Grant remembers in *Fourscore:* "This shock affected me deeply. I realized too late, as many have done, that I

might have been more tender and more articulate as to what I was doing and thinking" (159). The next year, his father—then well into his seventies—failed in business, an event which left Robert "sick at heart, for I idolized him, and humiliated" (159).

But not everything was bleak. In the winter of 1878, Grant had been introduced to Amy Gordon Galt, who was visiting in Boston in the company of her father, Sir Alexander Tilloch Galt, whom Grant describes in *Fourscore* as "a prominent Canadian statesman" (133). Amy "was tall, spirited-looking, and very erect, with fresh color and brown hair rolling back from a noble brow" (132–33). Robert courted her assiduously in Canada and Europe, and although she refused him at first he became engaged to her in the fall of 1882. They were married on 3 July 1883 at Christ Church Cathedral in Montreal. They spent their honeymoon in the Adirondacks, Saratoga Springs (Grant recalls in *Fourscore* that he lost most of his travel funds betting on the wrong horse), and Nahant. After the summer season, the couple moved into "a snug little house" (166) in the Back Bay, 104 Marlborough Street. However, Grant's financial circumstances were not very reassuring: the annual cost of living came to approximately $7,000 (there were four maids and a chore man); the salary as the mayor's secretary stopped at the end of the year since Dr. Green had not been reelected; and Grant's other resources "consisted only of twelve hundred dollars income from my mother's estate and my contracts with James R. Osgood and Company" (160). Sir Alexander promised $1,000 annually but was unable to keep the commitment, although ultimately Amy received the money as part of her father's estate. Robert's father Patrick lived with the couple until his death in 1895 and shared expenses.

The King's Men

Keenly mindful of royalties now that he was married, Grant welcomed the offer of his "friend and fellow Papyrian, Charles H. Taylor, editor of the *Boston Globe*" (168) to participate in a novel to be written by four young writers. Besides Grant, these included Frederic J. Stimson and Jack Wheelwright—his friends from his *Harvard Lampoon* days—and John Boyle O'Reilly, another member of the Papyrus Club. Uncomfortable with the serious problem novel,

Grant—together with Wheelwright—succeeded in making the
novel a work of the lighter vein, although its dramatic plot is serious
enough as it incorporates some of O'Reilly's personal experiences as
an Irish nationalist. To quote from *Fourscore:*

There are already in print a number of authentic accounts of how as a
Fenian he enlisted in the British army for the purpose of inducing Irish
soldiers to revolt; of how he was detected in 1866, tried for high treason,
sentenced to be shot; of how the sentence was commuted to penal servitude
for twenty years; and of how with the aid of a priest (and as some said,
the jailor's daughter) he escaped in a boat from Banbury, West Australia,
in February, 1869, was rescued by an American whaler and carried to the
United States. (171–72)

The King's Men: A Tale of To-morrow is set in the future; the dates
are somewhat confusing, but essentially the action takes place in the
1960s. [12] Britain has been a republic for seventeen years: King George
V lives in exile in Boston's South End. But the republican government has also deteriorated; a Radical, Mr. Bagshaw, is now president. Other political factions are the Liberals, whose leader is
Richard Lincoln, and the Aristocrats (Loyalists), whose leaders are
Sir John Dacre and Colonel Arundel. A party at Ripon Hall in the
English countryside brings together Sir Geoffrey Ripon, who has
been living in what was the porter's lodge; the rich American
Abraham Windsor and his daughter Margaret (Maggie), who have
rented Ripon Hall; Mrs. Oswald Carey (Eleanor Leigh), with whom
Ripon was in love at an earlier time; Sir John Dacre; and various
other figures. Maggie and Ripon try to rekindle their romance of
two years ago when they met in Paris, while Dacre reveals to Ripon
a plot to overthrow the government and reinstate the king.

Both developments are foiled by Mrs. Carey. She tries to regain
Ripon but is rejected—not, however, without being observed by
Maggie in what seems to be a compromising situation with Ripon.
Overhearing Dacre's talk with Ripon, Mrs. Carey steals the list with
the names and details of the plot and goes straight to London to
inform Bagshaw. Naturally, the plot fails; Colonel Arundel is shot
and everyone else taken prisoner. Too late do Ripon and Dacre
realize the folly of their plan: King George is lily-livered and ab-

sconds from his secret quarters in London with Mrs. Carey after being warned by her that the gig is up. And too late—in the face of the firing squad—does Dacre recognize Mary Lincoln's love. Mary dies upon his execution; later, her father sees to it that they are buried next to each other.

For Ripon and most of the others, it is fifteen years of Dartmoor, but he and two fellow prisoners escape through the exertions of the Wilsons, with Ripon's servant Reynolds acting as the loyal messenger and helper. Back in Boston, Mrs. Carey completely dominates the king until her hopes to marry him are exposed. Ripon and his associates come to Boston to settle accounts with the king. Mrs. Carey tries to make things up with Ripon but is once again rebuffed; she leaves for Brazil with the man who revealed her queenly hopes to George. Ripon and Maggie finally fall into each other's arms, marry, have a son—Abraham—and return to Ripon Hall. Better times arrive for Britain also when Richard Lincoln becomes the revered prime minister.

This production of four authors is remarkably even in style and tone; it has far greater unity than Mark Twain's and Charles Dudley Warner's *The Gilded Age: A Tale of To-day* (1873), which is its model not only by similarity of subtitle. There are strong parallels between Eleanor Carey and Twain's Laura Hawkins, the trial scenes, and the general interplay of sentimental and political material in both novels. *The King's Men* does not have a Colonel Sellers but abounds with the kind of plot complication and satire so evident in Mark Twain's contemporaneous *Adventures of Huckleberry Finn* and the slightly later *A Connecticut Yankee in King Arthur's Court*. One of the most Twainian touches in *The King's Men* is the day of reckoning in Boston: in a scene both moving and farcical, the king ceremoniously holds drawing room in his second-rate South End hotel only to be mortified by the entrance of Ripon and his friends. This George V is first cousin to Twain's king and duke.

The King's Men is not the *Silas Lapham* type of novel the book's sponsor was hoping for, in part because Grant himself saw to it that humor and not seriousness prevailed. Grant thought that it "was not a good novel," but neither is *The Gilded Age* if judged by Grant's standard. In any case, doing his share of the book put Grant back on a successful track while at the same time deepening his feeling for political matters. *The King's Men* is strongly democratic yet informed by civility toward the former (i.e., then current) ruling class in Britain. Although the Mary Lincoln episodes are too melodramatic, characterization and dialogue are on the whole vivid and tasteful. High political adventure and conventional love story are combined into a very readable yarn, providing the additional advantage to Grant of establishing a lasting connection with the publishing house of Charles Scribner's Sons under whose imprint most of his later work was to appear. [13]

The Knave of Hearts

With *The Knave of Hearts: A Fairy Story* (1886), Grant returns to the theme and style of *The Confessions of a Frivolous Girl* and *Oxygen! A Mount Desert Pastoral*. [14] Young Arthur Lattimer of Boston is told by his great-great-aunt Selina not to marry hastily. She had in her youth given her heart to one Captain Michael Westering, but the captain was apparently lost at sea. He had given Selina a trinket in the shape of a human heart as a token of his love. She now gives this heart to Arthur, along with "a lancet in the form of an arrow. Its point was the blade, and the shaft, which was of raised silver, terminated in a minikin of a cupid after the manner of an apostle spoon" (23). She had herself received this lancet from the captain's family after they had accepted his fate. Selina, who is portrayed as an amiable old crone with not a small hint of witch, tells Arthur to bestow only a piece of his—and that—heart where he would impulsively give all.

Following her advice, Arthur goes through six acquaintances, three of which are described. The first encounter is with Blanche Lombard, a buxom giggly blonde whose fascination is girlish, physical, and domestic. The pleasant but shallow Blanche is followed by highly sentimental May Corcoran, who in turn gives way to Virginia Langford, a consummate Southern belle. Virginia represents high-class romance and queenly love but is abandoned by Arthur when she mentions that the disease of consumption runs in her family. Getting somewhat older, balder, and paunchier, Arthur repairs once more to Bar Harbor. There he discovers in dead Selina's papers evidence that Westering had betrayed her. Apparently destined to bachelorhood forever, Arthur Knave of Hearts concludes of himself and Selina that "we had given our hearts away and received nothing in return, though hers had been bestowed in one sweet breath, and mine doled out by inches" (174). Miraculously though, he meets there Westering's great-granddaughter Mabel, who drops an umbrella over the cliff; when he picks it up he sees "a minikin of a Cupid precisely similar to the device which adorned my ci-devant lancet" (176–77). No sooner are the reader's hopes raised than Mabel and Arthur discover that both of them have gone through the identical procedure of bestowing portions of their hearts. Now they are unable to love; their hearts are gone, and they must go their separate lonely ways.

It would be natural for the story to end with Mabel and Arthur falling into each other's arms (and their rhetorical exertions not to do so border on high comedy), but by the unhappy ending Grant saves the story from turning into mere formula fiction. What the ending also does is to negate the book's subtitle: *The Knave of Hearts* is not a fairy story, for lack of a happy ending and a serious quantum of fantasy. Though a very light romance bordering on the overly bittersweet and sentimental pulp literature, the book shows Grant's genuine ability as a satirist: May Corcoran is modeled after Royall Tyler's Maria in *The Contrast* (1787), and the scenes between her and Arthur make for some exquisite camp, including parodies of Tyler's "Son of Alknomook" and Edgar Allan Poe's "The Raven" (1845).[15]

A Romantic Young Lady

A Romantic Young Lady (1886) expands the fashionable society novel, of which the title is a good indication, into the novel of manners. The result is an entertaining and illuminating account of a young lady's growth from "innocence" to "sophistication" to "(un)common sense."[16]

Like Alice Palmer in *Confessions,* Virginia Harlan, the heroine, tells the story herself. Her father, Augustus Harlan, is a Boston railroad magnate too busy to be bothered with his daughter's upbringing. Since her mother died at Virginia's birth, the girl is raised under the tutelage of two feuding spinster aunts, the intellectual Agnes and the home-body Helen. Private school proves too much for Virginia's health, and she gets a somber but competent governess instead: Miss Jenks teaches her the values of intellectual discipline, order, and thoroughness. Virginia regains her health, becomes well-educated, but also tends "to introspection and over conscientiousness. I picked up pins, and went out of my way to kick orange-peel from the sidewalk, on principle" (11). Caught in this narrow existence, Virginia turns into a dreamer: "I liked to picture myself in some of the romantic situations of which I had read, and to build castles for the future." Her dreams are not specific but give her the delicious "consciousness of a great possible happiness" (12).

Hermetically shielded, Virginia grows up without knowing that she is an heiress, without forming any friendships with girls of her age and class, and without any contact with boys. She also grows up to be very handsome. Her father gives her some advice—she must learn to be independent and make her own decisions if she hopes to be happy—and $100,000 in stocks to manage on her own so that she may know about matters of business and property, normally considered to be beyond a woman's range. Although Virginia now feels "a new responsibility in living" (19), it is no surprise to see her fall in love with the first man who pays attention to her. Romantically, they declare their love at a summer resort, only to run into stiff opposition by Virginia's father. He characterizes Roger Dale as a flighty man about town without means, ambition, and character but a keen eye for the main chance. When he vows to disinherit his daughter, leaving her only the stocks he had already given her, Virginia puts all her trust in her lover and, to Dale's dismay, throws the securities into the ocean. True to the father's prediction, Dale loses no time in backing water, and the engagement is broken off.

Virginia of course is crushed but recovers with the help of her father. Her greatest need now is "to meet and know a different set of people from those of the fashionable world" (80). At her aunt Agnes's, she meets the social gossip columnist Lucretia Kingsley who introduces her to a group of bohemians and their spiritual leader Mr. Spence. Initially, Virginia does not recognize the vapidity

and fatuousness of this circle. She believes in Spence, whose guru
attitude she mistakes for true spiritual capacity and devotion to a
higher principle, and becomes treasurer of his Society for the Practice
of Moderation. An absurd though passionate declaration of love by
a painter associated with the group is followed by Spence's own more
moderate one. She does not love him but considers his offer because
of her other needs. Once again, her father helps her make up her
mind. In the most serious conversation of the entire book, Grant
strikes up the theme which will from here on inform all his writings.
Virginia's father apologizes for his shortcomings, his neglect of
Virginia because of his business: " 'In this country, we most of us
have only time to get together our millions and die. . . . But we
expect our children to make a good use of the leisure we have won
for them' " (203). It is no longer a matter of her learning to manage
a certain amount of money; what Augustus outlines is a succession
of roles and responsibilities within the growth of American civilization: " 'I could tell you how to make money, and how to keep
it, perhaps; but how to spend it wisely requires a different sort of
talent than I possess. I have told you, from the first, that it was to
be your life-work' " (205). He regrets the indulgence with which
his daughter has been brought up to have her own way like all
American women. Virginia counters that ever since childhood she
has been alone and left to her own responsibility. She will not take
Spence, but she once again implores her father to guide her, to take
the burden of responsibility from her. Instead, her father takes
himself away from her: he dies of a heart disease which he has had
for some time, and leaves her sole heiress to four million dollars.

But Virginia is not totally alone. Horatio Chelm, her father's
legal adviser, is helpful in the management of her fortune, and her
aunt Helen comes to live with her. For three years, Virginia keeps
to herself except for being active in charities, but then she is per-
suaded to give a large ball which turns into an initiation into her
real world; she finds many serious, good people among the rich
whom she had thought frivolous. Thus, her education continues:

It was clear to me that earnest-minded people existed among the very
wealthy no less than among those less fortunately circumstanced; and as
this grew more apparent, I began to catch a glimpse of what my father

had meant in speaking of wealth as the power and possibility of the world. Was it not essential to leisure; and leisure to refinement and culture? And where necessity ceased to control action, ought there not to be a greater chance for excellence and progress? (232–33)

To learn more about and keep active in this new world, Virginia, encouraged by Helen, forms a salon.

Meanwhile, fortune enters Virginia's life from another direction: a certain Mr. Francis Prime of New York City walks into Chelm's office to ask for advice. His father has lost his fortune through misplaced confidence; he himself is a perfect gentleman, but one who cannot find anything to do. Chelm explains to Virginia that, at the present time, gentlemen without independent means do indeed not have a fair chance in this democratic society, primarily so on account of their forefathers who " 'have a heavy score against them in the past' " (260). Here is someone of her own class, able apparently to do something with money—an art the cultivation of which Augustus Harlan had enjoined on his daughter. Virginia's interest is awakened; she directs Chelm to set up Prime as a banker with $250,000 of her money. Foolhardiness or deeper knowledge? Chelm's doubting admiration hints at another theme Grant will be developing in his subsequent novels: " 'The whole scheme is the most Utopian I ever heard of. These women, these women! It makes a prudent man tremble to think what would become of the universe if they had full sway!' " (260) Explaining the proposition to Prime, Chelm invents a hilarious story about a sixty-five-year-old anonymous benefactress; Virginia's listening in on the conversation begins a series of complications with all the elements of Marivaux's comedies. [17] Virginia goes to New York to keep a side glance on Prime. But a new involvement appears to develop: she meets the Honorable Ernest Ferroll who will be duke of Clyde. One day, a policeman tries to arrest the disguised Virginia for loitering outside Prime's establishment; Prime defuses the situation and offers "Miss Alice Bailey" (315)—her identity is now doubly concealed—work as a clerk. She accepts, excels, and in due time draws a deeply felt, passionate declaration of love from her employer to which she listens with a rapture never known to her before. She tells Prime that she loves him but cannot marry him—it would be a misalliance (the reader here is able fully to enjoy his privileged position of being informed where Prime is ignorant); finally he agrees to let a year go by during which they will not communicate. Virginia is at the height of her powers; it seems to her as if she had never lived before; she even gets her aunts to be friends. Her father's notion of the power of wealth has now been complemented and completed: "The power of love, and the power of money! How when united did they each illumine the other,—they, the two greatest forces of the world!" (343).

The stage is set for a rousing denouement. Virginia's first lover, Roger Dale, fails in the amount of three million dollars. Prime is one of Dale's largest creditors and therefore also fails. He fails because, like his father, he places trust in someone who should be a gentleman but is not. Dale commits fraud; without telling Prime of his true state, he borrows from Prime over night only to suspend payment the next morning. Virginia comes to the rescue: Chelm tells Prime that he will be saved if he marries his benefactress who, so Chelm is instructed to admit, is not sixty-five at all but young and beautiful. Prime, of course, avers his constancy to Alice Bailey; Virginia is overjoyed to have found a true man, and all ends happily (the future duke of Clyde has found money elsewhere and returned to England). As in a fairy tale, Virginia's early dreams of "a great possible happiness" have come true.

If *A Romantic Young Lady* seems derivative in its basic outline— in addition to the eighteenth-century French comedy of manners of Marivaux there are echoes of the eighteenth-century English character novel of Richardson: Virginia Harlan resembles Clarissa Harlowe not only in name—its strength lies nonetheless in its particular American elements, chief of which is Grant's conviction that the day of the gentleman (and lady) is not only not over but more necessary than ever before. His view is strikingly parallel to that of John William De Forest who saw the salvation of postbellum America in "the worthy gentleman of democracy."[18] A romantic young lady no more, Grant's Virginia Harlan has found her place of power as a worthy lady of democracy, as Mrs. *Prime.*

Face to Face

Although Grant had been relieved to abandon the more serious work unsuccessfully attempted in *An Average Man* and to return to the lighter style and subject matter of *The Confessions of a Frivolous Girl* in *The King's Men* and *The Knave of Hearts*, the desire to write something successful outside his established line continued to urge him on to new experiments. He did not leave his accustomed terrain in *A Romantic Young Lady*, but he gave that book much greater depth than his previous ones by carefully developing the theme of initiation and the study of manners. Even while he was at work on *The King's Men* he had begun *Face to Face*, which he "resolved to publish anonymously in order to ascertain whether I could not attract notice by a novel written in the third person and a more serious vein without being detected."[19]

The daughter of a wealthy English banker of ancient lineage, Evelyn Pimlico insists on doing things differently. Instead of marrying into the peerage she goes to college; instead of rejoicing at Queen Victoria's taking the title empress of India she voices anti-establishment sentiments. When Willoughby Pimlico invites one of the honorable's daughters to visit New York, Evelyn's father decides to send her in order to have her cured of her newfangled notions by exposure to the radicalism he believes to be rampant in the United States, and in order to land perhaps a rich son-in-law. Evelyn, however, is fiercely and comically pro-American and most eager to go for quite different reasons of her own. Sailing by accident without a companion and dressed in what she believes to be the latest American fashion, Evelyn soon gets entangled in a comedy of errors on board ship. Wishing to teach him a lesson, she scrapes acquaintance with a young man whom she considers one of "the gilded youth of the United Kingdom" (36) and annoys him by playing the part of an American girl. Mr. Ernest Clay objects to her Daisy Millerism; he believes her to be from the West. He himself is no Englishman but a New Yorker of excellent family, education, and means. Somewhat of a dandy, he is as Anglophile as Evelyn is Pro-American. In a rousing speech, Evelyn attacks Clay's cultural defeatism:

"Is it possible . . . you believe that the great Republic of free men and women over there is to become nothing but a gorgeous reflection of the virtues and vices of an out-worn hemisphere? You seem to forget the world has opened its eyes at last to the fact that the rights and sufferings of common humanity have a greater claim on its consideration than the prerogatives of kings. How shall I and my brother man live more happily, more wisely, more truly, is the heart whisper of millions to-day who never saw the 'peerage' and have no ideas of precedence. To this end all earnest men and women are devoting the energies of life. And yet you would persuade me that this is but a phase soon to be, if not already, lulled to sleep by the twin narcotics, luxury and conservatism." (72–73)

In New York and later in Newport and Lenox, Evelyn is disappointed that America is not and does not wish to be socially and culturally different from the Old World. Ernest Clay, on whom Evelyn has made a great impression despite her deliberate lack of social graces on the *Britannic* (he would not take any other steamer!), meets Evelyn again, and Evelyn's American host Clara Pimlico urges her to be receptive to Mr. Clay's attentions: " 'You should look at the world as it is, my dear, and not as you imagine it to be' " (145). Subsequent discussions between Evelyn and Clay on the subject of America not only change her view of him somewhat but develop at some length the problem of the new American leisure class of which Clay is an outstanding example. He has six million dollars, all the amenities and advantages, yet—as he says himself—he amounts to nothing. " 'What is wanted are not lawyers and merchants, but souls not afraid to run amuck with society as it exists, with the hope of changing its current' " (183). But where to find something really meaningful to do? Clay has no answer for himself, and Evelyn cannot offer one either; quite to the contrary, it is Clay's honesty which destroys her own sure notions and makes her see the complexity of " 'the world as it really is' " (185). Clay also deplores the failure of the women of the American leisure class to motivate the men by setting " 'the standard of living high' " (188) instead of being content with vanities, a remark not lost on Evelyn.

Clay is in love with Evelyn, and Clara Pimlico urges Evelyn to consider marrying him. Her arguments are very sensible and practical, and Evelyn admits that in matters of matrimony too her notions might have been wrong. A letter from her mother informs her of heavy financial losses her father has just had and suggests in a postscript " 'that you would do well not to discourage any young man who may happen to take a fancy to you merely because he is an American' " (220). Evelyn is keenly aware of her responsibility toward her unmarried sisters. Her dreams are shattered: "And now she had come to herself and was face to face with the real world once more—the practical world, as her cousin Clara called it, which was the same everywhere" (221).

Face to face with the necessity of making a good match, Evelyn searches her soul. Although she likes Clay she does not love him, and she fears the kind of life he himself had described to her. She decides to use her college education and work instead of marry. She thinks she might begin by being a private teacher. Clara, of course, is horrified, and the entire plan is postponed when Mr. Brock, the man who was to escort Evelyn on the *Britannic,* invites her to visit him at Highlands, his country place on the Hudson River. As it happens, Brock's estate adjoins Seven Oaks, that of the Clays. Brock and Clay have controlling interests in two mills in the valley, and it is through this configuration that Grant introduces the element of labor and its leading exponent Andrew De Vito. The illegitimate son of a "gentleman" and an Italian working woman, De Vito has coarse though manly features, a strong build, poor manners, but a high degree of intelligence. De Vito is the spokesman and leader of the striking mill-workers, and although Brock and Clay are impressed by his speech and privately concede the justness of his demands that the workers share in the profits, they yield to the hardline approach of the mills' superintendents. De Vito's bitterness and class-consciousness erupt at a chance meeting between him and Evelyn. Later that evening, the conviviality of Brock's party is interrupted by De Vito's staring at Evelyn through a window. In a discussion with Clay, Evelyn feels great sympathy for De Vito's lot, but Clay is too wrapped up in his personal suit for her to offer more than commonplaces on the question of rich versus poor. However, he recognizes in her a finer courage than he himself has been able to muster and pays her a high compliment: " 'It is you who are the American. The seed sown by my ancestors has been blown across the ocean and has taken root on foreign soil; and now you appear as its representative to teach me what I ought to be' " (267–68). He already represents the power of money, but when he asks Evelyn to join him in the power of love, she refuses because she does not love him: " 'Our work lies before us. Our paths must divide for the present' " (276). Reflecting on the turbulent developments since she first set foot on America, Evelyn recognizes that "money was the most precious gift of matter, and love the noblest representative of spirit. In the union of these two mighty forces was the hope of civilization, the promise of the progress of the race" (280). Sadly, too, she realizes that the union of these forces eludes her at this time.

Events continue in rapid succession. Evelyn is attacked by a burglar in Brock's house; De Vito is suspected but later cleared. Most spectacularly, Brock dies and leaves his fortune of fifteen million dollars to Evelyn before she has a chance to start earning her living. In one of his last remarks to Evelyn, he sounds just like Augustus Harlan speaking to Virginia:

"If I had my life to live over again, I suppose I should act differently. I ought to have done more than I did. But you must remember . . . that I had my own way in the world to make. I had very little education, and I was over fifty years old before I had the leisure to consider such questions. Besides, at that age it is hard to adopt new ideas. But with you, my dear, it is different." (291)

So it is indeed. Evelyn sees her chance to do something different. She decides to manage Brock's Wisabet mill herself and invites De Vito to be superintendent: " 'Show me how the mill should be conducted so as to do justice to all' " (306). He accepts although he declares himself a radical, a socialist, who does not believe that her melioristic approach to do what is just and right will succeed. Under their direction, the Wisabet workers get better pay, share in the profits, and enjoy attractive housing. But after some three years have passed, the scheme becomes unworkable. Other mills, including the Clyme Valley mill at the same location (the one Clay principally owns), undersell the Wisabet because they produce with cheaper labor. De Vito invites her to concede the failure of her approach and to join him now as a radical union leader. But Evelyn " 'cannot bear to believe that there are no better remedies than resistance and retaliation' " (331). And as if on cue, a *deus ex machina* makes his appearance: just then Evelyn receives an anonymous letter containing the specifications for an electrical machine that will cut production costs in half and make the Wisabet highly competitive; the patent is in Evelyn's name. Filled with new hope and energy, she asks De Vito to continue with her in her way, for part of the blame for the condition of the poor rests with the poor themselves, and leadership must come—always has come—from the elite. De Vito, however, will temporize no longer: " 'It is too late. . . . The masses know their power too well to halt now. If you do not give, they will take. I am sorry to desert you, lady, but I warned you' " (341).

Ernest Clay returns from Paris; it is he who invented the machine that saved Evelyn. He also no longer owns any stock in the Clyme Valley mill. That mill has been ruined by the Wisabet, much to Evelyn's distress. There is considerable labor unrest in town, and De Vito is at the head of it. In a tense but melodramatic finale, De Vito comes to propose to Evelyn (whom he has loved from their very first meeting) just when she is expecting a visit from Clay who had admitted his role in the patent matter. She rejects De Vito and accepts Clay, who comes face to face with De Vito: " 'I'm capital and you're labor' " (377). Clay challenges the labor leader to show just what it is that he offers Evelyn—a question De Vito can answer only with a threat. The drunk and rebellious Clyme workers have heard that Clay is in town. They still believe him to be the principal owner of their mill, and they set out for Seven Oaks to confront him. Leaving Evelyn—against whom there is no ill feeling—at Highlands, Clay rushes to his estate only to find that the mob is beyond appeal to reason. Seven Oaks is set afire, with Clay and his old servant Gregory trapped on a balcony. The sight of Evelyn rushing to Seven Oaks on horseback awakens De Vito from his frenzy; he is sorry that he egged on the men in hopes of revenge on Clay. De Vito gives his life to save Gregory and Clay whom he has to force to leave the balcony " 'for *her* sake' " (393) before he starts to do so himself but falls to his death when part of the burning house collapses. Evelyn and Clay attempt in vain to save De Vito's life but it is because of him, literally and figuratively, that she can say to Ernest: " 'We have our lives before us' " (396). Lives, clearly, to be devoted to the great goal she lectured Ernest on while crossing the ocean, not to the "twin narcotics" of "luxury and conservatism."

Although Grant does not provide a blueprint for progress of this kind, he has established a new sense of purpose and responsibility for the leisure class. Money and love are joined and, in Grant's words, what might they not accomplish together? Published the same year as *A Romantic Young Lady*, *Face to Face* is a decisive step beyond Virginia Harlan's story toward a view of the leisure class rather different from that which Thorstein Veblen would offer thirteen years later in his classic *The Theory of the Leisure Class* (1899). In both novels, benevolent elitism is the keynote, and as in *A Romantic Young Lady*, Grant spends much time and effort on characterization of milieu and people and on some fanciful plot complications. But much of the light social tone yields to the addition of two major concerns: the international theme, and the conditions under which the workers of America exist and, in fact, support the leisure class. Thus, the book's title has more than one meaning: dream and reality, England and America, capital and labor all stand face to face.

In a lucid though excessively deprecating passage on the novel, Grant—pleased and amused at the same time—comments on the interest the book created: "What all the reviewers stressed was the evidence of a more serious purpose, a compliment which, tickling my vanity for a moment, looked hollow on examination." Contrary to the reviewers' assumptions, "De Vito's personality and tirades contributed nothing to economic thought."[20] Grant concludes:

What *Face to Face* really taught me was that I could hold the public's attention by a story not couched in autobiographical form, and also that my portrayal of the social scene was none the less veracious for more careful workmanship and some toning down of my exuberances. The essence of the novel from a literary angle was still a comedy of manners in my own walk of life. The "serious" portion, though melodramatic in spots, was virtually padding.

It is difficult to take issue with the author's modest and frank evaluation, yet it seems necessary to suggest that the "padding" is responsible for the improved quality of his comedy of manners and therefore quite indispensable to it.

Mrs. Harold Stagg

Between critics' praise and his own strictures of *Face to Face,* Robert Grant seemed unsure of the direction he ought to take in his next novels. *Mrs. Harold Stagg* (1890)[21] and especially *The Carletons* (1891) are comparatively timid books and, though well-written, fail to reach the mark of *Face to Face.* This is not to say that they are mere potboilers: Grant continued to explore societal changes and to formulate and express his personal values and views of life. In *Mrs. Harold Stagg,* a novel named for the stagnating, reactionary power in the book, he interests himself in the new possibilities of women who unlike Virginia Harlan and Evelyn Pimlico are not heiresses. He adds a touch of regional and class contrast without making undue generalizations.

Harold Stagg is a wealthy New York banker; he leads an appropriate life which is categorically presided over by his wife Emma. They adopt the orphan children of Harold's brother Silas. Harold goes to Illinois to take Eleanor, aged eighteen, and her younger brothers Silas and Harold back to New York. Their small-town background does not overly worry the banker: "Emma would understand exactly how to transform this inconspicuous cygnet into a dazzling swan" (33). Eleanor, however, does not wish to dazzle; she does not want to "come out," but Emma insists. Grant emphasizes that Eleanor's reticence does not come from any notion of aggressive populist democracy, as Emma Stagg fears for a moment; Eleanor's scruples are not "born of that dreadful democratic spirit which argues that a country schoolma'am without social experience is the peer in breeding and elegance of any lady in the land" (52).[22]

After the coming-out ball, young millionaire Owen Page pays serious attention to Eleanor. Discussions generally introduced by Emma quickly reveal Eleanor's total lack of sympathy with the course of action prescribed for a New York debutante. Eleanor wants to do something useful in her own right: " 'I was brought up with the idea that I should have to work, and the thought of it has always been a joy to me' " (99). At the apartment of her uncle, Eleanor meets William Struthers, a promising young scientist. She admits to herself that Struthers is far more interesting than Owen Page and the other young men of her acquaintance. She repeats her intention of becoming a teacher and eventually perhaps a college professor. Her liking of Struthers actually sharpens her view of the development she owes to herself and society. Purely defensive at first (" 'But a woman can't afford to throw away her whole future merely in order to be married. Why should a woman give up her lifework more than a man?' " [147]), she finds her way to a balanced and persuasive outlook:

"Surely, uncle, it is not reasonable that I should have to pass some of the best years of life in idleness and amusement in order to keep myself before the eyes of young men who are on the look-out for wives. . . . I do not think a woman ought to consider marriage in such a connection. If men seek her out, and she loves one and is willing to forsake her work in order to be his helpmate, well and good; but she should make them seek her out and should follow out her own wishes and tastes just as if men did not exist, instead of sacrificing everything else in order to flaunt herself perpetually before them, as much as to say: 'I am of marriageable age and ready to be married. What do you think of me?' " (162)

She objects to the marriage market championed by the likes of Emma Stagg without relinquishing the feminine prerogative of being courted. Struthers declares his love, but the most she will do for him at this point is to assure him that she does not love Mr. Page either.

Five years elapse. To Emma's chagrin, Page has not persevered but married some other girl instead. Eleanor has an impressive academic career: teaching history and literature at Clavering College in Hoadley, Illinois, she has risen from tutor to assistant professor to—at age twenty-five—president. On their way to visit Eleanor, Harold and Emma Stagg disagree completely on her life: " 'Not one girl in a thousand would have done so well.' " " 'Not one girl in ten thousand would have wished to' " (198). Struthers too has made progress. A professor now himself and an electrical engineer, he has invented a profitable storage battery. He asks Eleanor to marry him. Though he would move to the college, she has to decide between him and her own promising career. She chooses him, but Emma is not pleased: after all, she could have made a brilliant New York marriage. To the last, Emma is unhappy, because Eleanor wants to be married at the college, not in New York.

Harold Stagg, then, was wrong in predicting that Emma would make a dazzling swan of Eleanor, but Emma's position and power are still formidable at the book's end. She will not be converted to Eleanor's ways of doing things: " 'It is perfectly certain that she and I are fated never to agree on any possible subject—never—never—never!' " (238) Little has been gained from the liberation of woman from the marriage market pattern as long as matrons like Mrs. Harold Stagg hold social power. Grant makes it very clear that it is not the men who are reactionary: next to Emma Stagg, both her husband and Struthers—not to mention Eleanor's uncle—are positively enlightened people.

The Carletons

Unlike Arthur Lattimer of *The Knave of Hearts,* Grant himself had bestowed his heart wholly and in time. By 1887, the Grants were the parents of three boys. Quite naturally, Robert's interest in fictional topics begins to shift from courtship to family life in the years after his marriage. Thus it is no surprise that in *The Carletons* (1891), his last novel before becoming a probate judge in 1893, Grant chronicles the life of a representative American family in the mid to late 1800s.[23]

John Carleton and his wife Mary live at Highlands, their homestead in Hampton, a rural community some twenty train minutes away from the city to which John commutes to run his lumber partnership. His is a familiar American story; he "was a country lad who had left his father's farm, like many before him, to seek his fortune in a city. After an apprenticeship of half a dozen years in a counting-room, he had started out in the lumber business on his own account, about the same time that he happened to make the acquaintance of the deacon's pretty daughter" (8–9). John and Mary have five children: William, Benjamin, Constance, Violet, and

Harold. John fights in the Civil War as a Union volunteer; after his return from the war, the family moves to the city for the benefit of the children's formal and social education.

The children grow up knowing the usual joys; grief enters their lives when their father dies. Bill joins the lumber business. Ben has artistic ambitions and eventually turns into a promising illustrator and cartoonist. Constance develops anemia, goes to Europe with her mother, and finally marries Percy White, a childhood friend she had rejected earlier. Violet becomes a hospital nurse and marries her childhood acquaintance Harrison Fay. Bill does likewise in marrying Ethel Davis who had refused him previously. Harold inherits money from Cousin Rebecca, loses it as a broker, and ends up with a job on the western railroad for which Percy White works.

The last chapter, "Happiness Galore," nicely sums up Grant's values as well as the changes likely and desirable to occur to young people of that time. No engagement or marriage takes place until the respective parties have matured, tasted work in the outside world, and established themselves as competent and independent people fit to raise a family. If nothing else works, the young man goes West, where he does a good deal better for himself than do Twain's and Warner's young men of *The Gilded Age*. However, it is not enough to prosper in business. John and Mary realize the value of a college education for their children. Bill, who does not take advantage of the parental offer, proves the point: " 'I'm a good business man, Violet; but what else am I? If I had gone to college, I might have been a good business man and something beside' " (283). Mrs. Short, a friendly neighbor, has the final word on woman's role; she tells Constance that " 'woman's real place is at home after all, and those of us who stray outside are to be pitied rather than congratulated' " (233).

The Carletons, although often schematic, shows Grant moving farther away from the position of satirist in the direction of novelist of manners. Here is a book perfectly expressing the circumstances of a typical ("John" and "Mary"!) WASP family: they are not rich but comfortably well-to-do, not always happy but never unendingly miserable. They lead an unspectacular but full and diversified life. Grant tunes his style well to the heights and shallows of the

Carletons' experience. Occasionally he manages to give a particularly
vivid picture, such as the description of Violet's grief after being
rejected, or the description of Highlands, which is the quintessential
Currier and Ives.[24] It is a book well balanced between disappointment and hope, grief and joy; the happiness detailed at the end of
the book in a long letter from Constance to her mother has a degree
of alienation as its corollary: the family is spread far apart all over
the country, and old Highlands itself has been torn down and cut
up into building lots, signaling the modern American life-style of
mobility and suburbia. But in the final analysis, what is the more
the same the more things change is the family as the basic unit of
American civilization; foreshadowing the Chippendales, the Carletons increase and multiply.

Chapter Three

Essays and Miscellaneous Works (1887–1912)

In *A Romantic Young Lady* and *Face to Face,* Robert Grant's interest shifted from the description of fashionable life to the study of social change and the resulting responsibility of the leisure class. *The Carletons* concluded his first phase as a novelist; his next novel *Unleavened Bread* did not appear until 1900. It is evident that *The Carletons* does not advance Grant's development as a serious novelist of manners. Rather, in its safe retreat to the American family, it signals his unwillingness or inability to continue at that particular point in his career in the direction set by *Face to Face.* His comment on *Face to Face* reads almost like a retraction of having introduced grave matter into a light genre. *The Carletons* seems not so much an expression of Grant's desire to keep himself busy while the well is filling up again as of his need to pause for awhile, to take stock, and to clarify his powers and ambitions as a novelist.

There were other, more mundane reasons for Grant's temporary withdrawal from the serious novel. His marriage in 1883, the birth of four children in the next few years, the consequent need to have a sufficient and permanent income all drew his attention away from larger issues to the everyday cares of a family man. After some thought he turned down an excellent offer from a manufacturing company in Manchester, New Hampshire: his father, who was living with his son's family, balked at leaving Boston, and ultimately Robert Grant himself decided that he too would not have been happy elsewhere. He was appointed a water commissioner in 1888 at an annual salary of $3,000, which was somewhat less than half of his annual living expenses. Grant had interest income from such capital as he had inherited, but the sum was not very large; until his appointment as judge of the probate in 1893, he simply needed to derive a good part of his income from his writing. He managed to do so quite nicely. Drawing on his experiences as a husband and father, a club man and a sports enthusiast, a proper Bostonian and an enlightened though conservative citizen, he wrote a great number and variety of popular books for boys, short stories and essays, all of which detail the lives and problems of—and therefore primarily found their audience in—people like the Carletons: "pretty good people," as he chose to call them.[1]

Two Books for Boys

Invited by Eben Jordan to write, for a fee of $5,000, "a book descriptive of the life of an American boy," Robert Grant responded with *Jack Hall or The School Days of an American Boy* (1887) and, when Jordan asked for a sequel, with *Jack in the Bush or A Summer on a Salmon River* (1888).[2]

Jack Hall. Jack Hall is a Beacon Hill orphan whose father died in the Civil War and whose mother does her best to bring him up the right way. The Halls are a proper Boston/Salem family going back "very nearly into Mayflower times" (29). Tradition is evident not only through place and parentage but also through class distinctions, exemplified in a snowball fight between the patricians who are led by Jack and fight like "grenadiers" and the plebeians (the "muckers") who are led by Joe Herring, a butcher's boy. Reminiscent of a similar scene in *The Education of Henry Adams,* the description of this battle is accompanied by Attwood's illustrations clearly portraying one group as upper class and the other as a pack of Dickensian rabble.[3]

At other times, Jack and his friends commit petty vandalism, probably for lack of proper opponents, and it is the frequent recurrence of broken streetlights and tricks played on the corner grocer which leads Mrs. Hall to send Jack to Utopia, a boarding school for boys some five train hours from Boston. The school's principal is Dr. Meredith, "a man in the prime of life, not quite forty, tall, stalwart, and commanding, with a sunny smile but firm mouth," a man, in short, about whom "there is nothing small and petty" (150). This father figure and role model loses no time in explaining to Jack and his friend Frank Haseltine what they have come for: " 'You have been sent here to learn to become high-minded, upright gentlemen, with lofty aims and sterling good sense in the first place; in the second,—and without this the first can never be completely realized,—to acquire a good education by means of faithful study. Intelligent scholarship is the promoter of many virtues and the key to success in after-life' " (157). To these excellent principles is added a "clean and neat" environment, including the food: "No extravagance, no rich dishes, no wine or beer, but plenty of blood-making, sinew-strengthening, bone-building food, fresh, appetizing, and unspoiled" (184). A judicious mixture of learning and athletics is to ensure healthy minds in healthy bodies for the ultimate benefit of civilization:

"This idea, boys, of becoming easy-going and nothing else is a very unfortunate one to entertain, especially in our country, where every man is expected to contribute in some way toward making the world more civilized, and a sweeter, happier place to live in. We need today the services of keen, disciplined minds in active life, and in its quiet walks those who love learning for her own sake, and are ready to devote patient days to the pursuit of ripe scholarship." (233)

For a time, this sort of sentiment is so much Greek to boys in or just past puberty. Jack, Frank, and two other boys form a gang, "The Big Four," complete with rules signed in blood: fun straight from *Tom Sawyer* and *Huck Finn* (their master's name is Sawyer!) which ultimately gets out of hand when they blow up the tool house. Initially, Jack is the only one who admits to the horrible deed. He receives a public whipping, and Meredith finds occasion for another speech: " 'What is most threatening to-day in the outlook for the noble development of this great democratic country of ours is the tendency to condone too easily embezzlement, breaches of trust, bribery, and other forms of public and private dishonesty, the kernel of which is deceit, and in the fostering of which lies national ruin' " (303–4).

Thanks to this lesson and the friendly guidance by an upperclassman who is both a distinguished scholar and successful athlete, Jack becomes a responsible youth interested in study and athletics. Despite only average ability, he manages by dint of perseverance to acquire a reputation as a well-rounded man. Soon he is acknowledged as one of the leaders of the school, and his great personal triumph comes when he wins an exciting single skulls race against an older student and Dr. Meredith who had never before been beaten at Utopia. A year later, Jack graduates third in his class and takes a prize for a translation of a poem by Ovid. His friend Frank Haseltine, whose father has suffered financial ruin, is a crack pitcher and receives an offer to play professional baseball, only to turn it down when a patron comes forward with the classic solution of the Gilded Age, a chance on a railroad out West. Jack will enter Harvard and can be counted upon to make just such a contribution to society as Meredith's early speeches called for.

Grant dedicated this book to his three infant boys, and a number of authorial intrusions as well as thinly disguised speeches on educational philosophy suggest that he was here projecting a system of education superior to that of the Boston Latin School where he had been a pupil and whose 250th anniversary in 1885 he had commemorated in a poem which mixed praise with criticism.[4]

Jack in the Bush.   A confirmed outdoorsman, Grant kept fishing for salmon in Canada until late in life, bicycled through much of France with his wife, and generally advocated physical exercise. *Jack in the Bush* distills this outdoors philosophy, with a dash of boy scout ethics, in the manner of Captain Mayne Reid's hugely popular books.[5]

Two experienced woodsmen, John Holt and Colonel Russell, take six boys to summer school at Gaspé Basin. Athletic Jack Hall is the book's hero, but his disdainful boyish confidence is balanced by the growth of Max "tenderfoot." After early attempts by Jack to humiliate the unathletic Max, the two are sent out together and quickly run into adventures which draw them closer together. Jack wounds a bear which turns on him, but Max risks his own life to save Jack and kills the animal with his knife—a feat of courage everyone had thought impossible for someone like Max to accomplish. Jack, of course, apologizes to Max for the nasty treatment he had given him earlier. A little later, the two boys give chase to the flambeauing half-breed Pete Labouisse. They chase him over the dangerous Injun

Falls; Pete founders but Jack saves him. Finally, the two men decide to have the boys choose by ballot who should have the camp's grand prize, a new rifle. Jack and Max tie; Jack wins the ensuing target shooting contest, but Max also shoots very well. At the end, the book's key message "Nature is God's best interpreter" has thoroughly worked upon the boys, and even Pete seems willing to mend his unlawful salmon-spearing ways and to "set up as an honest cobbler" (372).

The didacticism is heavy-handed to be sure; still, Grant succeeds in putting together a lively story which is relatively free of pathos. It is marked by a genuine love of the wilderness, a sincere wish to have boys learn and respect nature's ways, and a strong sense of comradeship.

Coasts North and South

Though primarily a salmon fisherman, Grant was interested and experienced in other kinds of fishing as well. A fine example is his piece "Tarpon Fishing in Florida" (1896).[6] He gives an account here of his trip to the Gulf of Mexico south of Tampa in March 1889 to fish for *Megalops thrissoides* or—more poetically because of its lovely silver scales—"Silver King." The tarpon is a huge fish beside which "the lordly salmon seems to sink into insignificance" (182). It seems almost impossible to land fish this size by way of a rod, and indeed tarpon fishing is still such a new sport that no generally approved and successful techniques exist. After some disappointments and a three-hour battle which gives him raw and bloody hands, Grant finally catches a six foot, one hundred and thirty-two pound tarpon who "was by far the most beautiful specimen of the fish creation I have ever seen" (216). Combining ichthyological, piscatorial, and geographical information, Grant's piece reads like a story out of today's *National Geographic*; despite its comments on the local arrangements, it is never in danger of deteriorating into tourist office style. Through it all swings the excitement of real sport, noble game, and impressive nature, and one is willing to accept Grant's conclusion that tarpon fishing is "the most magnificent fishing-sport in the world" (217).

In the opposite direction and much closer to home lies the North Shore of Massachusetts.[7] His brief piece on the North Shore is one in a series called "American Summer Resorts" which includes descriptions by other authors of Newport, Bar Harbor, and Lenox. Grant, whose grandmother owned a cottage in Nahant, is most qualified to write about "this paradise" because he is a member of the society which owns that coast, because he is aesthetically alive to its grandeur, and because he is hygienically and athletically enlightened to favor the physical exercise and sports which characterize it in contrast to the fashionable but essentially vapid spa life of, for example, Newport. Waxing poetic as he describes the seascape, Grant muses about the potential destruction which the leveling tendencies of democracy may bring at a future time, but for now he is happy reflecting that "the beautiful seaside estates which have been cut out of the coast-line from farthest Maine to the limits of the shore of Buzzard's Bay, during the last twenty years, are among the most precious of human possession, and that the class of people seeking for them is increasing in direct ratio to the growth of refined civilization over the country" (62–63). Thus Grant repeats once again his belief that the crude money-making ability of the American people must be and is being transformed into a cultured money-spending ability to advance the course of America's civilization to ever higher accomplishment.

Two Volumes of Short Stories

By the end of the nineteenth century the short story was such an accepted genre and so suited to and popular because of magazine publication that it is no surprise to see Robert Grant try his hand at it. However, he never seems to have considered the short story as more than a convenient outlet for material not suitable for a novel. The surprise is the popularity his stories did enjoy. Collected in two volumes, most of them appeared under the titles of *The Bachelor's Christmas and Other Stories* (1895) and *The Law-Breakers and Other Stories* (1906).[8]

The title story of the first volume concerns a well-to-do bachelor who plays Santa Claus to everybody and who in his loneliness decides "to give an entertainment to all the old bachelors and maiden ladies of my acquaintance" (33). His own lady love appears, clears up their misunderstandings, and accepts him because he finally proposes. "An Eye for an Eye" is a poignant account of a nun who commits perjury to ruin the future of the man who had rejected her. Her erstwhile lover goes to seek his death in the Franco-Prussian War, and she nurses him after he receives a mortal wound at Gravelotte. Though essentially a humorous tale, "The Matrimonial Tontine Benefit Association" is similar to "An Eye for an Eye" in Grant's refusal to allow money and career to triumph over love. "In Fly-Time," "Richard and Robin," and "By Hook or Crook" are undistinguished potboilers, with the final story marred by an anti-Italian slur.

The title story in *The Law-Breakers and Other Stories* takes up one of Grant's pet peeves, the habit of returning American tourists to cheat the customs, and overdevelops it into a point of character. George Colfax, a "passive reformer" (3) who "voted right, but, beyond his yearly contribution of one dollar, . . . did nothing else but cavil and deplore" (4), is in love with Mary Wellington who wishes to find out whether "his moral perceptions" are "genuinely delicate" (10). Returning from a voyage, Colfax and a Miss Golightly bribe the customs officials, whereupon Mary rejects him as unworthy. The next story, "Against His Judgment," also makes a point, but it does so with a touch of the relentlessness which marks Ambrose Bierce's best work. A crossing guard in Pennsylvania is killed snatching a toddler from the railroad tracks. George Gorham declares that the guard made a mistake, since his heroics left his family without its head. A year later, Gorham wins a young lady who in a discussion on the subject had come to his aid regarding the guard's action. On the way home, Gorham quite automatically saves a ragged urchin on a railway crossing at the cost of his own life and a happy future marriage. "St. George and the Dragon" is a piece directed against obnoxious sensational newspaper reporting. "The Romance of a Soul" is the story of a woman whose dreams of a Sir Galahad never materialize and who fails to receive the appropriate recognition for her selfless devotion as a teacher. "An Exchange of Courtesies" is a highly contrived love-and-money story set in a New England sea resort, but it contains an admirable portrait in the manner of Sarah

Orne Jewett and Mary Wilkins Freeman of two elderly sisters who
refuse to sell their small but superbly situated property to a newly
rich furniture magnate. "Across the Way" rewards with true friendship and love a virtuous, principled orphan girl who sets up as a
school teacher and refuses a chance inheritance. Finally, "A Surren-
der" answers the question "Should a man sell himself for the sake
of those he loves?" in the affirmative: a devoted scientist marries an
attractive and strong young widow who accepts him in full knowledge of his poverty but later persuades him to become a partner in
the bank of a friend.

One cannot improve on Grant's assessment of his own stories as
undistinguished work.[9] Wisely, he did not pursue the short story
further, despite the indulgent critical acclaim bestowed on his two
volumes by leading newspapers. To the development of the American
short story Grant added little if anything; his bleak record is bright-
ened somewhat by an occasional touch of genuine art, but there is
not one among his stories which deserves to be remembered today.
The short story simply was not for him; he was far more comfortable
and artistically successful with the novel and the essay. It is this
latter genre which constitutes the significant part of his literary
output aside from his novels.

The Reflections, Opinions, and Convictions of
Robert Grant, Essayist

The Reflections of a Married Man.   *The Reflections of a Married
Man* (1892) is the first in a series of chatty volumes of domestic
essays centered on the life of "Fred" and "Josephine."[10] It is an
amusing, good-humored account of the trials and tribulations of
marriage and keeping house, of the joys and woes of bringing up
children and fulfilling a definite role in society. Spanning only five
years, it still presents a full record of Grant's basic view of life. This
view has its self-deprecating and humorous elements: " 'And have
you ever thought, Fred,' said Josephine to me one day, 'that we
suddenly awake at forty and realize that we are just the sort of people
we intended not to be?' " (179). That sentiment, however, quickly
resolves itself into a generally optimistic view that such is life and

that the world is moving forward. Fred philosophizes: " 'I flatter myself that we are a little more liberal, a little truer-hearted, a little wiser than our progenitors, just as our children are likely to be an improvement on us if pretty good people are not swept away in the deluge of democracy' " (180–81). But Josephine has of course the last word, which conveys more than a mother's solicitude for her children's welfare: " 'I only hope, Fred, that they will be happy as we have been' " (181).

The Opinions of a Philosopher. The sequel, *The Opinions of a Philosopher* (1893), reassures the reader that the four children— Fred, David, Josie, and Winona—do have their fair share of happiness, but otherwise the message becomes more serious.[11] Taking the family fortunes up another fifteen years to Fred's and Josephine's silver anniversary (Fred is now fifty-five), humorous episodes such as little Fred's football heroics at Harvard and Josephine's efforts to save Fred from the rut of middle-age alternate with Winona's attempt to practice Christian Science and Fred's unsuccessful bid for Congress. Observing changes in American life and ideals, Josephine and Fred worry about "Whither is civilization tending? What is one to think of it all? And by the shades of my forefathers, purified by pie, how shall we best help our sons and daughters to hitch their wagons to stars?" (65). Simplicity has given way to "the virtues, tastes, and vices of the other nations against which our forefathers barred the door" (63). Most unsettling is "this whole business of the emancipation of woman" (119). Fred expostulates on this theme at length:

To realize her progress, I have only to glance up at my ancestor with the mended eye and consider what a doll and a toy she was to him. Then I look at my wife, who was brought up on the old system, and say to myself that, unless, indeed, man is to be utterly snuffed out and extinguished, there are certain feminine characteristics in the preservation of which he is deeply interested, even when, like myself, he is at heart an aider and abettor of emancipation. No more gingerbread education, no more treatment as dolls and nincompoops, no more discrimination between one sex and the other as to knowledge of this world's wickedness, no more curtailment of personal liberty on the score of that bugaboo, propriety—all these, if you like, ladies; but we men, we fathers and philosophers, ask that you retain, for our sakes, beauty of face and form, beauty of raiment, low, modulated voices, and a graceful carriage, faith, hope, and charity, even though you continue to reveal these last-named as at present with sweet, illogical inconsequence. More than this, we cannot do without the tender devotion, the unselfish forethought, the aspiring faith, which, even though we seem to mock and to be blind, saves us from the world and from ourselves. If you are to become merely men in petticoats, what will become of us? We shall go down, down, down, like the leaden plummet cast into the depths of the sea. We shall be snuffed out and extinguished in sober truth. (151–52)

Earnest convictions in a playful, still slightly condescending guise: but in this selection are foreshadowed the themes and boundaries of Grant's major novels from *Unleavened Bread* to *The Dark Horse*.

   The Art of Living.   *The Art of Living* (1895) is a collection of informal papers on the pattern of the Fred-and-Josephine essays.[12] There is very little in these papers that Grant does not discuss elsewhere, either in his novels or in his nonfiction, and one suspects this book to be a potboiler, written on a successful formula with a slightly changed focus and identity ("Barbara" and "I" instead of Fred and Josephine).

   Successively, the items under discussion move from the most mundane ("Income," "The Dwelling," "House-Furnishing and the Commissariat") to the most philosophical ("The Case of Man," "The Case of Woman," "The Conduct of Life"), but the abstract and the concrete are mixed throughout. Thus, the paper on "The Dwelling" includes a consideration of specific houses as well as general considerations of changing housing patterns (including apartment dwellings and suburbs), domestic service (maids or housekeepers are hard to get), and architecture ("Our national house architecture may be said to be working out its own salvation at the public expense" [59]). This rather free-wheeling pattern serves Grant's persona of the bourgeois social critic well, although it offers little excitement for the reader. Discussing house-furnishing, Grant reviews the standard commonplaces of American civilization (imitation of Europe's taste, the glory of the American bathtub, the negative effect of the new immigrants); he concludes with a complaint which sounds very modern indeed: "Here there is perpetual waste—waste—waste, and no one seems to understand how to prevent it" (106).

His chapter on "Education" criticizes the attitude of the well-to-do who profess "that our public schools are the great bulwarks of progressive democracy" (108), only to send their own children to private boarding school. Somewhat at variance with Grant's views in *Jack Hall,* this discussion reveals much of the imitative social class thinking which fosters an elite essentially alienated from the job of making the everyday world of democracy better all the time. This great goal is, however, advanced by making education available and attractive to women, a topic upon which Barbara discourses at some length.

Reviewing available careers, the chapter on "Occupation" points out that military, clerical, and intellectual careers in general are more highly respected and more plentifully available in Europe than in America. Fairly disillusioned, Grant points to the stockbroker and the journalist as typically American professions and suggests that once again democracy ought to set its sights high. "The Use of Time" is a plea for something more than the energetic, restless work which characterizes Americans. On a hopeful note, Grant insists that "the interests of the average American are much wider and more diversified than those of any other people" (190). In particular, the American hunger for knowledge is commendable, but here as in social life, "moderation and choice" (209) must guard against excess or mere quantity.

Two papers on man and woman review the social and legal status of woman, the historical domination of man, and the current advocacies of change. Grant is uneasy with the lack of direction the emancipation movement shows, although he sympathizes with woman's desire to have her innings for a change. His tone fluctuates between the intensely interested and the patronizingly biased. Clearly, he is uncomfortable and generally upset over the topic, and his definitions and suggestions with all their rhetorical triteness do more to identify sides than to offer solutions: "The point of the argument is that the dependence of each sex on the other, and the loving sympathy between them, which is born of dissimilarity, is the salt of the human life" (304). "The true mission of the modern

woman," Grant feels, "is to supplement and modify the point of
view of man, and to extend the kind of influence which she exercises
at home to the conduct of public interests of a certain class"
(310–11). How these interests and class arrange themselves within
a democratic society is not discussed much beyond an almost frantic
invocation of the "eternal feminine" (315). In contrast to his subsequent novels on the matter of marriage and divorce, Grant's
thoughts in *The Art of Living* are little more than a barometer of the
unsettled and unsettling social climate in which he finds himself
as a man, a husband, and a judge.

The final chapter on "The Conduct of Life" grows into a *Summa*
of Americanism: "What do we stand for in the world?" (321) Sin-
gling out Lincoln as "undoubtedly the best apotheosis yet presented
of unadulterated Americanism" (327), Grant defines the concept as
a combination of naturalness, self-respect, desire for self-improve-
ment or success, energy, and self-reliance. He deplores the threat
posed by the huge immigration of "riff-raff" (335) and adds racial
slurs which would later call in question his impartiality in the Sacco-
Vanzetti case. Grant's perfect America is ultimately his own: of
Anglo-Saxon stock, with high ideals but committed to the idea of
democracy. It is a nation guided by—as he calls them in *The Reflections of a Married Man*—pretty good people. "The art of living
is the science of living nobly and well" (350–51), and the ultimate
goal of American democracy is to be a light to the world.

Search-Light Letters.   The third of the Fred-and-Josephine
essay volumes, *Search-Light Letters* (1899), is not a record of the joys
and sorrows of some pretty good people but four series of letters,
somewhat on the Chesterfieldian model, to various correspondents—
letters distilling political and social wisdom and nobility.[13]

The first series, four letters "To *A Young Man or Woman* in Search
of the Ideal," starts out with certain assumptions about the recip-
ients: assumptions, essentially, about their sterling qualities of character, their wish to become "uncommon" (3) persons, and their
belief that, as Fred the philosopher puts it, "The homely adage that
you cannot make a silk purse out of a sow's ear is full of meaning
for democracy. Manners must go hand in hand with morals, or
character will show no more lustre than the uncut and unpolished

diamond, whose latent brilliancy is marred by uncouthness, so that it may readily be mistaken for a vulgar stone" (2–3).

Quite literally then, Grant is not concerned with the "swinish multitude" but the elite. In an extended railroad metaphor reminiscent of Hawthorne's celestial railroad and De Forest's train of human progress, Grant distinguishes between first-class and second-class passengers.[14] The self-centered, refined lady of "personal culture and individual salvation" (22) joins a variety of other people in second class, because she—as do they—lacks the proper balance between individual and social responsibility. To be first class, a passenger must cherish and maintain "the noblest aims of the aspiring past" in the sense of a "broader humanity" (58).

"To *A Modern Woman* with Social Ambitions" is not addressed, as the designation might imply, to the woman's libber but to the happy wife and the contented spinster "without a grievance against Cupid" (62) who "are simply eager to help in working out the problems and fulfilling the destinies of your native civilization with benefit to society and credit to yourself" (67). Reviewing the hoary problems of "no standards in this country" (93) and of being democratic yet maintaining "the old standards of elegance and refinement" (109), the series concludes with a panegyric suggesting that woman's true identity is and always has been not that of the independent antagonist of man but of the great civilizer, all the more so since she is now no longer in bondage:

Clearly, the modern woman with social ambitions must not neglect to hold fast to the old and everlasting truths of life in her struggle toward the stars. Sympathy with and capacity to promote new ideas are essential to her progress, but only by allegiance to the eternal feminine, to the behests of love and motherhood and beauty of imagination, can the development of society on the lines of a broader and wiser humanity be effectually established. (124)

"To *A Young Man* wishing to be an American" defines Americanism as a "consciousness of unfettered individuality coupled with a determination to make the most of self" or "a compound of independence and energy" (125). Fred reaches back to what Grant was to call "the white light of Concord philosophy" in *The Chip-*

pendales: to Emerson ("hitch your wagon to a star") and Thoreau ("simplicity"). He has little sympathy with Daisy Millerism or other proverbial aspects of American innocence abroad; in his view, "our national life has become both complex and cosmopolitan" (127–28). There is a list of "those who are not true Americans" (135): "the plutocratic gentleman of leisure who amuses himself" (135; this category includes ladies too); "the easy-going hypocrite" (139), and "the worshipper of false gods" (wealth; 146). Reiterating all the shopworn phrases of a century of American independence, Fred sets up universal progress as the hallmark of successful Americanism ("if our nation is to be a lamp to the civilized world" [134]), adds a bitter drop by naming an Englishman, Rudyard Kipling, as the writer who "has more clearly and forcibly than any one else expressed the spirit of the best Americanism—of the best world-temper of to-day" (169), and gives an expanded definition of the true American: "It is incumbent, therefore, on you, if you would be an American in the best sense, to fix your ideal of life high, and at the same time to fix it in sympathy with the underlying American principle of a broad and progressive common humanity, free from caste or discriminating social conventions" (159–60).

Finally, "To A Political Optimist" gives the reason and need for Fred's advice. A bitter satire on political corruption in American cities culminates in this kind of judgment: "The unwritten inside history of the political progress of many of the favorite sons of the nation during the last forty years would make the scale of public honor kick the beam though it were weighted with the cherry-tree and hatchet of George Washington" (219). Not all is well in America, and *Search-Light Letters* is an attempt by Grant to reach out to the audience of his earlier Fred-and-Josephine books in order to activate them, because "there will be leading villains and low comedians so long as society permits, and so long as the conscience of democracy is torpid" (233). A firm belief in traditional values, in progress, in the American world mission combines with the pride and zeal of the political and social reformer and the sometimes chatty, sometimes didactic voice of the philosopher into an uneven but sincere and moving appeal to all good Americans to come to the aid of their country.

The Convictions of a Grandfather. Although Fred and Josephine appear in *Search-Light Letters,* it is *The Convictions of a Grandfather* (1912) which properly concludes the "Fred and Josephine" series.[15] Because the cohesiveness of the family as an organizational pattern for the book is necessarily not nearly as strong as in the earlier volumes, Grant's topics range rather widely from an update on Fred's and Josephine's children and grandchildren to a discussion of the modern woman in general and the American woman in particular, and on to old age pensions, workman's compensation, and progressive inheritance tax. The final third of the book turns into an increasingly bitter reckoning with the moral and aesthetic vulgarity of modern American democracy and its self-complacency. A journey by chauffeured car through England affords Fred and Josephine an opportunity not only to see new sights and to reminisce about a much earlier lovely bike trip through France (and a not so pleasant Italian journey), but more importantly the chance to expose "democracy's—and especially American democracy's—indifference to background" (277). This highly autobiographical account thus turns into Grant's opportunity to air grievances of long standing: "background" means ancestors, history, taste, "romantic sensibility" (285), in short, precisely the kind of cultural leaven which Grant had hoped was being genuinely desired by American democracy as it prepared to leave the shirt-sleeved Gilded Age and assume world leadership. For Grant—as for Henry Adams—the European cathedrals symbolize the grandeur of a tradition which, if it cannot and should not be resurrected, still serves as an undeniable challenge to the modern progressive age: "When will democracy, the spires of whose cathedral are the yearnings of the common heart, its cornerstone the brotherhood of man, evolve the genius which will interpret once more to the outer eye in transcendent terms of artistic beauty its sound but disillusionizing creed?" (287).

Summary.   Grant's five essay volumes from 1892 to 1912 range widely in form and theme. The organizational pattern of *Reflections, Opinions,* and *Convictions* is defined by the essay persona— the couple Fred and Josephine—and their successive circumstances and experiences. It is a most successful pattern, for it accommodates any topic with the greatest of ease: things simply happen in the life of Fred and Josephine as naturally as the seasons come around. *Humani nil a me alienum puto* could well be Grant's motto as essayist:[16] no topic is too small and none too large to touch the life of Fred and Josephine or their children or their grandchildren. From whooping cough to woman's emancipation, from football to freedom, from drawing room to democracy—all is fair game for the essayist.

As is evident in the titles, Fred is the chief spokesman, but Josephine's views are also clearly heard. There is no need for a subdivision of these three books into particular areas or groups of topics; they are divided into chapters, but only for mechanical convenience, and they are therefore not titled but only numbered. Fred and Josephine are a typical upper-middle-class couple in whom any upper-middle-class reader of the period is apt to recognize himself; his problems tend to be theirs also, and his experiences are mirrored in theirs. The distance, to use Arthur Miller's term, between the author's persona and the reader is minimal, partly because of their similarity of situation, partly because of the style. Grant is a master of the informal, conversational, chatty style which invites and inspires closeness and confidence. It is no surprise that these volumes were highly popular and served to some extent a "Dear Abby" function: the right kind of reader felt himself touched and comforted and aided.[17]

The three volumes chronicling the life of Fred and Josephine are masterpieces of the domestic sketch and the essay of manners. In their own way, they form a series in the tradition of Oliver Wendell Holmes's "Breakfast Table" books. To be fair, Grant was not "A Leyden-jar always full-charged, from which flit / The electrical tingles of hit after hit," but he was no dead battery either.[18]

As Fred ages, his reflections solidify into opinions and finally harden into convictions. It is toward the end of *Convictions* and in the more formal *The Art of Living* and *Search-Light Letters* that the domestic sketch and essay of manners give way to the didactic and moralistic essay, a development reflected in the separately titled chapters and narratively rather self-contained papers of the two books between *Opinions* and *Convictions*. In his fear that the course of American civilization might go awry, Grant increasingly drops the familiar pose and becomes preachy. He does offer solutions, but they seem paternalistic and limited to his own class, to the "pretty good people": the concept of democracy as the Founding Fathers defined it must be kept alive during the Gilded Age and after. In particular, the new immigrants of non-Anglo-Saxon stock must be brought to understand, revere, and emulate this ideal—that is, the very people who are most easily distracted and corrupted by materialistic expectations and machine politicians. Grant's strongest appeal is therefore to the leisure class, which must exercise leadership. As in *A Romantic Young Lady* and *Face to Face,* salvation lies not in conspicuous idleness but in conspicuous responsibility on the part of those who are in a position to do something significant. Together, *The Art of Living* and *Search-Light Letters* come very close to a Handbook of Good Citizenship.

On the whole, Grant was quite pleased with his essayistic work. Sometimes controversial, often conservative, always entertaining and instructive, it was widely read and well received.[19] Grant had clarified for himself and his readership just where he stood: in analogy to those members of the leisure class who frittered away their time and talent or gave in to cultural pessimism, Grant too could not continue to serve up tentative opinions in pleasantly satiric but essentially shallow novels of fashionable life. Ten years after *Mrs. Harold Stagg* and *The Carletons,* the time had come for a truly serious major novel.

Chapter Four

The Benham Novels

Water Commissioner and Judge of Probate

During the 1880s, Robert Grant had made great personal and literary strides; he had married and become a family man, and he had begun to make a name for himself as a writer. What he had not achieved by the end of the decade was professional and financial stability. He had rejected an offer to become associated with *Life* in New York City and another offer to become an attorney for a corporation in New Hampshire. For some time he had a minor function in the office of Charles Pelham Greenough, a prominent lawyer who encouraged Grant's literary activities and furthered his legal career by having him "chosen secretary of the Bar Association of the City of Boston when he declined re-election in 1886."[1] Soon afterward, two of Grant's friends of the Papyrus Club, O'Reilly and Taylor, intervened with Mayor O'Brien in Grant's behalf when a position on the city's Water Board became vacant. Grant "was at a loss to know why the Mayor should have consented to nominate one who knew nothing of the water system or mechanics and could be of no assistance politically" (172). One should indeed have expected the position to go to one of the mayor's Irish friends; that it went to Grant instead was evidence of O'Reilly's and Taylor's influence, not—as Grant briefly thought—of a need for "a respectable dummy over whose eyes the wool might be astutely pulled" (172). Grant soon discovered that technical knowledge was neither required nor really necessary, since the city engineer and his subordinates were in charge of technical details. What was necessary was "honesty and sound judgment (which often meant mere commonsense)" (174). Grant found much of the work boring, but his "New England conscience" (176) made him do his duty faithfully.

The position was valuable for the annual salary of $3,000 it carried, but there were side benefits: Grant had enough time left to continue to write, strengthening his ties with *Scribner's Magazine* and "its accomplished and ever helpful editor, Edward L. Burlingame"; furthermore, "the training I received during these years in the rough-and-ready of life was just the tonic that my diffident personality stood in need of" (179). Having survived a change in the mayor's office, Grant became chairman of the board in 1890. His greater visibility made his job uncomfortable at least twice: once when the town of Quincy objected to the laying of water pipes and Grant barely managed to avert a bloody scuffle between Quincy and Boston workmen, and another time when he had to testify in the matter of a contract and lost his temper when confronted with an outright lie.

Grant had turned down the New Hampshire offer primarily because he could not bear the thought of leaving Boston, "the modern Athens where I knew all the passwords" (167). What the passwords meant in practical terms became clear very soon afterward. Nathan Matthews, the third mayor to hold office during Grant's tenure on the Water Board, was "a friend from boyhood," and Robert was therefore "in clover" (175). But matters improved beyond Grant's feeling secure in his commissionership. During the 1880s he had come to know William E. Russell, a rising politician of his own set; when Russell was "elected Governor in 1890, we had been friends for half a dozen years" (190). In 1893, the Massachusetts legislature established "a second Judge of Probate and Insolvency for Suffolk County" (191). Grant had the support of the governor and of leading members of the Boston (Suffolk) bar, and even though his lack of legal experience and his career as a writer of light literature raised some questions about his suitability, he was confirmed by the Executive Council and assumed the new judgeship in July 1893.

From all points of view, knowing the password at this occasion was a stroke of luck for Grant. He writes in *Fourscore:* "For a number of years there had been at the back of my mind the inchoate belief that the dignified and sufficiently honorable post of Judge of Probate would suit me temperamentally and afford some leisure for literary work" (191). Although the legal work was not glamorous—"a Probate Judge was then associated in the legal mind with listening to old women and a not too profound mental capacity" (191)—the advantages of the position were obvious to Grant: he would be financially secure, and he "should be out of the whirlpool of competitive court practice, yet, as the umpire in a continual panorama of issues affecting welfare and property, see human nature at short range and try to hold the balance even between rich and poor, the humble and the great" (191). At long last, the early hope of being a writer, a man of letters, and a lawyer all at the same time had materialized.

Grant's life had taken a desirable turn, and even the death of his beloved father in 1895 did not stop its even and pleasant progress for long. A fourth son had arrived a few years before, and the Grants now needed a larger home. Robert used his inheritance from his mother, money which came to him after his father's death, to buy a house even farther away from Beacon Hill and downtown than his previous residence on Marlborough Street:

The Back Bay and the Fenlands, one merging imperceptibly into the other, are really one great flat region recovered from the swamps, the Fenlands possessing the great advantage of having a great part kept as parkways, with water and bridges. The residences of the Fenland are of a more interesting average than those of the Bay—and it is over here, in the Fen country, that Robert Grant the novelist lives, at 211 Bay State Road.[2]

Social life, especially the theater and the clubs, provided entertainment outside the house, but family life did not suffer. Robert and Amy and the older sons became expert bicyclers; bicycling was the fashion, and Robert recalls "encountering Justice Holmes on the mill dam in Boston. As we approached one another on the wooden bridge, I saw that he was grasping the handles of his machine as if it were a demon. Instinctively, I waved at him as we passed, with all the aplomb of an experienced rider, though with no *arrière-pensée*. He did not seem to notice me. A few days later I heard of his saying, 'Bob Grant waved at me from his bicycle, d—— him. The next chance I get, I'll overrule him' " (212).

Unleavened Bread

The 1890s were a very eventful decade for Robert Grant, but underneath the activities, pleasures, and distractions of everyday life, he kept his literary ambitions alive. His "heart was set on writing a significant novel of American scope," an "important" if not the "great" American novel.[3] Even while he was busy writing essays and short stories—in fact as early as the writing of *Mrs. Harold Stagg*—the most impressive figure he ever created began to take shape. After he had accepted the essentially repugnant nature of Selma White, his best novel, *Unleavened Bread* (1900), almost wrote itself. The actual writing took three years, but here for once was a novel which he did not have to worry into being.[4]

Beginning shortly after the Civil War, *Unleavened Bread* chronicles the emergence of a new American attitude, the Know-Nothing, populist mentality of the Gilded Age which seems—at least in literature—forever connected with the Midwest. Benham is its city and Selma White its high priestess. Grant details the life and career of Selma and marks the stages of her development by a steady increase in geographical perspective, cultural and social issues, and personal and political power. In making a woman rather than a man his—negative—chief character, Grant connects the political theme with the theme of women's rights. Appropriately, he discusses the three distinct stages of her evolution in three books successively named "The Emancipation," "The Struggle," and "The Success."

"The Emancipation." The very first chapter abounds in important expositional detail. It starts conventionally enough: orphaned, living at her aunt's farm, a country school teacher, Selma passes for the most intelligent girl in town and learns early to think for and about herself. When she accepts the proposal—fittingly made on a nighttime country road on the way home from a wedding—of Lewis J. Babcock of Benham, a good, sturdy but intellectually light-weight fellow who is rising in the varnish business, twenty-three-year-old Selma does so in the expectation of financial security and social advancement. She is eager to leave Wilton where, as the name suggests, she cannot blossom. It becomes clear, however, that the rural and geographical background signaled by the name of her native village of Westfield has conditioned her ideological perspective. While she accepts "Boston and New York and a few other places" as "authoritative,"

she accepted them, as she accepted Shakespeare, as a matter of course and so far removed from her immediate outlook as almost not to count. But Benham with its seventy-five thousand inhabitants and independent ways was a fascinating possibility. Once established there the world seemed within her grasp, including Boston. Might it not be that Benham, in that it was newer, was nearer to truth and more truly American than that famous city? She was not prepared to believe this an absurdity. (3)

Selma's personal and national definitions are similarly predetermined in the rough. "To be an American meant to be more keenly alive to the responsibility of life than any other citizen of civilization, and to be an American woman meant to be something finer, cleverer, stronger and purer than any other daughter of Eve" (3–4). There is nothing wrong with the sentiment itself; Grant had quite seriously detailed it repeatedly in his essays. What is worrisome is Selma's inability to fill the commonplaces with solidity or at least to raise them to a poetic, visionary level as Walt Whitman had done in *Democratic Vistas* with its inspiring though global and unspecified notions for America and a superrace of mothers.[5] Selma's "mission in life had promptly been recognized by her as the development of her soul along individual lines, but until the necessity for a choice had arisen she had been content to contemplate a little longer" (4). When Babcock asks her to marry him, all she knows is that "she was tired of her present life. What was coming would be better. Her opportunity was at hand to show the world what she was made of" (9). She wants Babcock to let her "do things" (6), but when he tries to find out what she means by this, she cannot elaborate beyond a firm yet dreamlike assertion of her personal ambition: " 'Yes, do something worthwhile. Be somebody. I've had the idea I could, if I ever got the chance.' Her hands were folded in her lap; there was a rapt expression on her thin, nervous face, and a glitter in her keen eyes, which were looking straight at the moon, as though they would outstare it in brilliancy" (7).

The wedding is only a formality legalizing her new position and status, not an event filling her soul and heart. Grant does not describe it but rather informs the reader in passing in the second chapter that it has occurred; he tucks it away as one line in a four-line sentence. The Babcocks live in a modern house on the outskirts of Benham, the kind of home Grant criticizes as an architectural aberration of the jigsaw run rampant: gingerbread, with colored glass touches, and a metal stag out front. Babcock is happy in a rather passive way, but Selma does not really enjoy his notion of a quiet home-life. She is conscious of not being at the top of Benham society; and even though this early she labels the high society people on River Drive "unworthy and un-American" (19), she is not satisfied with her present position. The Babcocks get involved in Episcopalian church work, and Selma is invited to the committee in charge of building a new church. Her initial leanings toward a local builder's design (he would give the varnish order to Babcock) are masterfully changed by the highbrow Mrs. Hallett Taylor, who quiets Selma's misgivings about European-style designs with an appeal to her intelligence and refinement—a compliment greedily devoured. Selma easily takes care of her husband: " 'I'm sorry about the varnish, but a principle is involved' " (35).

Mr. Wilbur Littleton of New York wins the competition, and Selma becomes "suddenly conscious that she had been starving for lack of intellectual companionship, and that he was the sort of man she had hoped to meet" (39). Even as an intellectual conversation between Selma and Littleton is interrupted by Babcock's arrival at home, so her hopes for a more stimulating life are dashed by pregnancy: "Her confinement came as an unwelcome interruption of her occupations and plans" (51). She gives birth to a daughter to whom she gives the sonorous name of Muriel Grace. She does not nurse the baby because she does not produce enough milk, but she transforms her physical inadequacy into an evolutionary triumph of the spiritual over the animalistic. Joining a literary club, the Benham Woman's Institute, Selma meets Mrs. Margaret Rodney Earle, whose marriage broke up because her husband objected to her living her own life.[6] Meanwhile, Littleton gets more and more absorbed in Selma and her "worried archangel look" (63). The church is finished to everyone's satisfaction, including Babcock's who gets the varnish order after all. Leaving the slightly ill baby under the maid's

care, Selma accompanies Littleton to the church for an inspection.
Littleton pays her high tribute. Conscious that he will come to
Benham no more, Selma feels self-pity on the way home: she has
come to the conclusion that she ought not to have thrown herself
away on Babcock. When she gets home, she finds chaos: Muriel
Grace is dying of membranous croup, and Babcock, beside himself
with grief, accuses Selma of having neglected the child. But she
calmly points out his error, and she allows herself to be reconciled
to her husband, of whom she is fond "as she might have been fond
of some loving Newfoundland, which, splendid in awkward bulk,
caressed her and licked her hand" (71).

The reconciliation cannot hide the fact that their marriage is
hanging by a thread. With baby gone, Lewis Babcock perceives *his*
loneliness, which Selma does nothing to alleviate. Consciously she
continues to live *her* life. When she goes—without her husband of
course—to a Women's Congress in Chicago, Lewis visits the country
fair with an old acquaintance; the two men get drunk and pick up
two women. One of them tells Selma, who thus gets the chance she
has been hoping for. And how the offended archangel cuts down
the fruitlessly contrite canine: " 'I went away for a week, and in my
absence you insulted me by debauchery with a creature like that.
Love? You have no conception of the meaning of the word. Oh no,
I shall never live with you again' " (79). It is a fine rerun of Mrs.
Earle's speech to her husband at the time of her separation, to a
dramatic rendition of which Selma had been treated early in their
acquaintance, but enriched by Selma's personal touches of grievance,
superiority, and historic mission. She wants no alimony; what counts
is that she is free at last. The minister of her church too finds that
her mind is made up. Mr. Glynn "trusted to what he regarded as
the innate reluctance of the wife to abandon the man she loved, and
to the leaven of feminine Christian charity" (88). But Selma is
unleavened bread, advising him that she does not love Babcock and
that " 'we American women do not feel justified in letting a mistake
ruin our lives when there is a chance to escape' " (89).

Escape she does. She gets the uncontested divorce but decides
"to retain the badge of marriage as a decorous social prefix, and to
call herself Mrs. Selma White" (90). She wants to earn her living

by doing newspaper work and to fix "attention on herself" (91). Before she gets really started (and disillusioned), Littleton comes to town on a further consultation with the church committee. Upon learning that Selma has been separated for six months and divorced for over one, he declares his love for her. Even while genuinely enraptured, she allows all the possible advantages of a marriage to Littleton to pass review before her mind's eye before she accepts his proposal, approving "her own sagacious and commendable behavior" (102). They are married on the spot, and once again there is no real wedding: "They were made husband and wife three hours before the departure of the evening train for New York" (105).

"The Struggle." Initially, provincial Selma is awed by New York. During her first few weeks in the city, she is timid and insecure, always on guard against the unknown and surprising. Observing everything around her, she becomes conscious that neither her wardrobe nor her bearing comes up to New York standards. Despite her instinctive clinging to populist views as a defense against a Europeanized life-style that is foreign to her, she ultimately decides to do as New Yorkers do. She begins to compromise on some of her notions, "for the leaven of the New York manner was working" (160). It was working so strongly that after a year and a half of marriage to Littleton, Selma considers that in Benham, as Babcock's wife, she never needed to worry about expenses, whereas now the cost of things and Wilbur's lack of wealth obstruct her ambitions. Her attitude sours; she quarrels with Wilbur's gentle and refined sister Pauline and feels "a sort of contempt for the deliberate, delving processes of the Littletons. She was inclined to ask herself if Wilbur and Pauline were not both plodders. Her own idea of doing things was to do them quickly and brilliantly, arriving at conclusions, as became an American, with prompt energy and despatch" (177).

After three years, Selma and Wilbur still have no children. Initially, Selma is sad indeed not to be a mother once again, but she soon decides that she has a different and perhaps more important function: she wants to provide the energetic management which she finds lacking in Wilbur's affairs but which seems necessary for him to become famous and wealthy. At this point, children would only be in the way. Relentlessly she pushes Wilbur into a more commercialized line of work which he resists because he cannot vulgarize his art, cannot sacrifice principles to expediency. She explodes and gives him a variation of her scene with Babcock: how she gave up *her* opportunities in marrying him, etc., and insists that she is in the right. Wilbur is nonplussed, shocked even, but tries to be noble. Their relationship is broken, although Selma rejects the idea of divorce or separation and continues to live in his house, intending "to enjoy her liberty at his expense" (236).

Selma has not come much nearer to defining the "things" she reserved the right to do when she married Babcock; as her quarrel with Pauline shows, she is firmly of the opinion that the true American need not train for anything in particular; all that is needed is the opportunity to show one's native ability. Just now, she craves the opportunity to be a leader of society, primarily on the strength of her excellent American convictions and her real or imagined intellectual and executive superiority. But society fails to take notice of her and to avail itself of her talents; deeply offended, Selma vents her ire at Flossy Williams, who cannot believe that the woman she had felt impelled to respect as an intellectual of high spiritual ideals turns out to be merely vulgarly jealous. In a blistering speech, Flossy exposes Selma's pretentiousness:

"I was saying that you were not fit to be a social success, and I'm going to tell you why. No one else is likely to, and I'm just mischievous and frank enough. You're one of those American women—I've always been curious to meet one in all her glory—who believe that they are born in the complete panoply of flawless womanhood; that they are by birthright consummate house-wives, leaders of the world's thought and ethics, and peerless society queens. All this by instinct, by heritage, and without education. That's what you believe, isn't it? And now you are offended because you haven't been invited to become a leader of New York society. You don't understand, and I don't suppose you ever will understand, that a true lady—a genuine society queen—represents modesty and sweetness and self-control, and gentle thoughts and feelings; that she is evolved by gradual processes from generation to generation, not ready made." (243)

Selma responds in kind:

"Yes, I am one of those women. I am proud to be, and you have insulted by your aspersions, not only me, but the spirit of independent and aspiring American womanhood. You don't understand us; you have nothing in common with us. You think to keep us down by your barriers of caste borrowed from effete European courts, but we—I—the American people defy you. The time will come when we shall rise in our might and teach you your place." (244)

After Flossy has left, Selma reflects on this extraordinary scene, only to emerge with the sharpened purpose "to have done with them forever, and to obtain the recognition and power to which she was entitled, in spite of their impertinence and neglect" (248).

Wilbur is chosen to build Wetmore College at Benham. Selma takes the opportunity to suggest that the only thing that is really wrong with their life is New York; she is convinced that they could be happy again if they went to live in Benham. But however congenial Benham might be to her, Wilbur recognizes it as—by comparison with New York—a cultural backwater. He rejects Selma's plea, even though he is kind enough to mitigate the refusal by saying that he cannot leave New York just now—perhaps later. Soon, Wilbur comes down with pneumonia. It is clear that major reasons for his collapse are overwork, worry, and personal unhappiness. Selma feels it to be her duty to nurse him, but once again her motivation is not selfless: it is her chance to prove her devotion to him and to turn his inevitable gratitude and appreciation into a general acceptance of her views and plans. She is offended when Dr. Page, a friend of the family, takes little account of her and calls in a trained professional nurse. She objects to Page's passive approach: fearing for Wilbur's heart, whose psychologically weakened condition he attempts to ascertain through searching questions directed at Selma, he prescribes no medication but only absolute rest. Selma longs to do something decisive: "It came over her as a conviction that if she were elsewhere—in Benham, for instance—her husband could be readily and brilliantly cured" (261). Wilbur dies, and Selma renders final proof of deserving Flossy's strictures when she all but accuses Dr. Page of malpractice: " 'I cannot believe that Wilbur's death was necessary. Why was not something energetic done?' " (263).

"The Success." Alone once again, with little money left by her husband but convinced that "the development of her own life was more intrinsically valuable to the world than his," Selma is determined to gain "due recognition" (265) from the world. She wants to go back to Benham and considers earning her living by acting or lecturing or reciting; she will do no more "subordinate work" (266). Wealthy Mr. Parsons's invitation to be his housekeeper and companion in Benham relieves her of any immediate material worries. During her New York years, Benham has continued its phenomenal growth, and she now returns there with high hopes. In comparison with her beginnings there as Mrs. Babcock, Selma too has made great progress: after all, Mr. Parsons has bought a mansion on River Drive, where Benham's aristocrats live. She is welcomed back by Mrs. Earle and other members associated with the Benham Institute and glories in the knowledge that they will eagerly honor her slightest wish for leadership.

Selma loses no time in aligning herself with the antiaristocratic faction against the Reform Club, an organization dominated by Mrs. Hallett Taylor and people like her. The first test case is the candidacy of Luella Bailey for the Benham school board. Miss Bailey is poorly qualified to be a school board member; she " 'hasn't had any special training, but she's smart and progressive, and the poor thing would like the recognition' " (274). It is clear that Selma champions her because she recognizes her alter ego. Despite strong endorsement from congressional candidate James O. Lyons, Miss Bailey is not elected, but the incident has sharpened Selma's outlook and made her acquainted with Benham's rising politician. A corporate lawyer of strong build and evident virility, a Methodist and a widower, Lyons expresses Selma's political convictions and appeals strongly to her imagination.[7]

Selma's life continues its familiar pattern. Wetmore College is rising, but it is in the hands of Mrs. Taylor and her high society friends. Selma would have liked to be a Wetmore trustee or even president of the college, a position which falls to Pauline Littleton. It upsets Selma that there already exists in Benham just such a dominating group as she had hoped to put together, and that this group completely ignores her. When Parsons becomes ill, she nurses him competently and gains his gratitude. Soon after, the dying Parsons invites Lyons to draw up his will; Selma will receive $20,000, but what makes her jubilant is Parsons's decision to give half a million for a free hospital. She immediately sees the hospital as her opportunity to exercise power and control, and she makes sure that Lyons, the executor of the will, gets the point that she wants to be on the board. In their fight against the elitist Reform Club, she learns from Lyons the value of practicing "proselytizing forbearance" (309) rather than "righteous invective" (304). She becomes the more stridently populist the more the aristocrats ignore her, and has the politically astute insight "that it would be an easy task to unite in a solid phalanx of offensive-defensive influence the friendly souls whom these people treated as outsiders, and purge the society atmosphere of the miasma of exclusiveness" (312). When Lyons proposes to her whom he considers a "mature, well-poised character endowed with ripe intellectual and bodily graces" (300), she does not repeat the mistake she made when she married Babcock and Littleton; this time, she names her price distinctly: " 'The knights of old won their ladyloves by brilliant deeds. If you are elected a member of Congress, you may come to claim me' " (322).

Lyons is elected, comfortably and by just such a phalanx as Selma had envisioned. Selma easily persuades Lyons that he should buy Parsons's house. In contrast to her first two nonweddings, Selma makes sure that her third becomes a well-publicized gala affair. Their wedding journey takes them not to Europe but to the American West. Selma has high hopes for their life in the capital; as a congressman's wife, she expects open doors in Washington. Her expectations seem initially to be fulfilled, but her eyes are opened at a White House reception. Selma realizes that she is overdressed, but as always she puts the blame on someone else, in this case those guests who do not seem to think that the American president is worth getting specially dressed up for. Flossy Williams tells her that in Washington political status does not automatically bring social status, and that the people who set the tone are " 'the nice people here just as everywhere else; the people who have been well educated and have fine sensibilities, and who believe in modesty, and unselfishness and thorough ways of doing things' " (353). When this verdict is confirmed by Mr. Horace Elton, a powerful man from their home state, Selma realizes that her hopes are dashed and "that Washington was contaminated also" (358). She still does not recognize her basic jealousy: "Even now had anyone told her that the ruling passion of her life was to be wooed and made much of by the very people she professed to despise, she would have spurned the accuser as a malicious slanderer" (360). Thus, she once again turns vindictive: "She would not forsake her principles. She would not lower her flag. She would return to Benham. Washington refused her homage now, but it should listen to her and bow before her some day as the wife of one of the real leaders of the State, whom Society did not dare to ignore" (360).

Lyons's rise to the desired position is rapid enough. He, a Democrat, and Elton, a Republican, make a deal: Elton will see that Lyons is elected governor, if Lyons will enable Elton to obtain a lucrative gas franchise. Lyons is elected, and Selma now basks in the limelight. She also takes satisfaction in the news that Flossy Williams's husband has failed through fraudulent speculations by his partner. But even her rise to first lady of her state does not solve her most urgent problem: "When she became the Governor's wife she had said to herself that now these aristocrats would be compelled to admit her to their counsels. But she found, to her annoyance, that the election made no difference" (402). Yet she gets all the exposure she craves in state-wide and national bodies and conferences. Then suddenly one day Senator Calkins of their state dies. Lyons's hopes to replace him hinge on his attitude toward Elton's gas bill. He must oppose it if he hopes to be elected senator, but of course it means not fulfilling his part of the deal with Elton. In a long conversation, Selma the red-white-and-blue archangel and perverter of Emerson's "Self-Reliance" destroys his scruples: " 'This is not a case of commercial give and take—of purchase and sale of stocks or merchandise. The eternal verities are concerned. You owe it to your country to break your word. The triumph of American principles is paramount to your obligation to Elton' " (425). What she really means of course is that he owes it to *her* to veto the bill. Again a critical point between husband and wife is reached, but Lyons is not Littleton, even though Grant makes him not entirely despicable. Selma reminds Lyons that her happiness, her life rides on his decision, and that they " 'are called to high office, called to battle for great principles and to lead the nation to worthy things.' " Expediency is declared " 'superior ethics' " (427), and Lyons dutifully vetoes the bill. Taken by surprise, Elton realizes that he cannot stop Lyons now and must bide his time to get even. Pledging " 'to remain a democrat of the democrats, an American of the Americans,' " Senator-elect Lyons delivers a rousing speech to which Selma listens "with a sense of ecstasy. She felt that he was speaking for them both, and that he was expressing the yearning intention of her soul to attempt and perform great things. She stood gazing straight before her with her far away, seraph look, as though she were penetrating the future even into Paradise" (431). It is still "things," "great" and "worthy" ones, just as she had equally vaguely hoped that night near Westfield when Babcock asked her to become his wife. But with a difference: then, she had been staring at the moon; now, her gaze has become millennial.

Selma. Readers and critics and Grant himself saw that Selma White was both a writer's triumph and trial. Midway between character and caricature, she is a type to be hated rather than a heroine to be loved: not unlike, for example, some of Molière's title figures. Grant did, in fact, originally consider "An Unconscious Hypocrite" as a title.[8] This quality may add an internal reason— to the external one of the novel's success—for its being made into a play, though it was a drama critic who pointed out Selma's essential weakness, a weakness Molière's characters do not have: she "is a mental treat but she is also an emotional chill."[9] Thomas Wentworth Higginson also put the case very well when he wrote Grant:

The character of Selma is as distinct a creation as that of Becky Sharp and as true to its surroundings. The physical type you attribute to her is admirably appropriate and she always fits well in her place. Her fatal drawback as compared with Becky is in being too absolutely repellent, whereas Thackeray saves Becky from this; first, by her humor which is a universal solvent and secondly by her willingness to do a good-natured act when it costs her nothing. This, I fear, is what will prevent the book from ever becoming popular in a permanent way.

What Higginson could not know was that merely by putting Selma in the neighborhood of Becky he paid Grant an extraordinary compliment, for Grant considered *Vanity Fair* "the greatest novel ever written."[10]

Bliss Perry made an equally flattering remark: "You have 'fixed the type' as irrevocably as Flaubert did in *Madame Bovary,* and I should like to overhear a heart to heart talk between Emma and Selma."[11] Grant does indeed use his wide reading to establish some similarities between *Unleavened Bread* and a number of European masterpieces, but a look at *Madame Bovary* shows that such parallels are mostly superficial. Like Selma, Emma Rouault is intellectually superior to her suitor Charles Bovary and marries him for no special reason. She, too, has a daughter whom she does not nurse and generally neglects. Grant uses Flaubert's technique of discriminating between actions of the mind and actions of the heart, but in contrast to Emma, who is passionate with her lover and heartbroken when he deserts her, Selma has little in the way of a heart. Thus, *Madame Bovary* takes a different emotional and narrative course, even though its subtitle "Provincial Manners" applies very nicely to at least the first book of *Unleavened Bread.* And its end is not at all to a "new" woman's liking, as one of the most emancipated young women in *The High Priestess* is gently advised.[12]

Selma's maiden name "White" suggests innocence but also the blankness of a page. She certainly is not Snow White, although she likes being fussed over; rather, she behaves like the queen, Snow White's stepmother. At a crucial point in *Unleavened Bread,* immediately after her no-holds-barred altercation with Flossy Williams, Selma "scrutinized herself eagerly and long in her mirror" (247): mirror, mirror on the wall, who is the ablest of them all?[13] But what answer can a mirror give? Selma does not consult people; they are interesting to her only as mirrors who confirm her self-image. She is narcissistic, a perennial adolescent. This quality is reinforced by her downplaying her femininity, by her recurring touches of frigidity, and by her thin lips and steely eyes. She does not seek the other person even though she is three times married. The only times she changes her mind are occasions on which she is either flattered (by Mrs. Taylor) or educated to a more promising

political strategy (by Lyons). Twice she is severely challenged, oc-
currences which she does not solicit and which she cannot handle:
she refuses to accept either Wilbur's or Flossy's criticisms and, quite
consistent with her nature, terminates the relationships. Selma's lack
of warmth and her basic state of nonpersonalization are graphically
rendered by her analytic habits and her reliance on ready-made
concepts and phrases. Her speech is sententious and unoriginal.
When she wants to move back to Benham, she does not think in
those words but rather in these: "She inclined toward Benham as
a residence" (265). The frequent phrase "she was pleased to" or "it
pleased her"—the impersonal version is more noticeable—rarely
indicates genuine pleasure; usually it is synonymous with "she
deigned to" and expresses condescension. Selma does not communicate.

Disquieting and destructive enough on the personal level, Selma's
narcissism is positively frightening on the political and cultural
levels. Democracy means the orderly give and take of a pluralistic
society, but Selma's idea of it has all the looks of an American
version of the dictatorship of the proletariat.[14] She is not a democrat
but a demagogue. Without batting an eye, she is absolutist enough
to create an identity chain that reaches from "I" to "we" to "the
American women" to "the American people," and she does so without Whitman's poetic though naive vision. In Selma and Lyons,
everything Henry Adams says in his novel *Democracy* (1880) about
political corruption is revived, and one remembers uncomfortably
that Adams's senatorial villain Ratcliffe is not only a thinly disguised
historical figure but also a midwesterner.

Another fairy tale analogy suggests itself: like the woman in
Grimms' story of "The Fisherman and His Wife," Selma does not
know what it is she really wants, except that she is dissatisfied with
what she has and that she must always have something bigger. Her
ideas do not grow in substance or specificity, only in size, a category
even Sherwood Anderson still characterized as quintessentially
American.[15] At the end of *Unleavened Bread,* unleavened still, she
is a senator's wife: what would she be next—the president's? And
afterward? The fairy tale has the fisherman's wife desire spiritual
power once worldly power is exhausted: after emperor comes pope,
which combines both powers and is a particular delicacy if seen in

terms of Selma's feminist activism; then the wish to be like God; then disaster. Hubris is the frightening implication of Selma's gazing as into Paradise and Flossy's imputation that Selma thinks of herself as flawless and ready-made as though she were Pallas Athene springing from the head of Zeus. One reacts to Selma's development and the fisherman's wife's in the same way: at first there is sympathy with their lot and a certain amount of satisfaction in their betterment ("Emancipation"), then questioning and antipathy at their growing selfishness ("Struggle"), finally disgust and fear at their triumphant dehumanization ("Success").

But the two stories do not end in precisely the same way, although similarities exist even here. Grant chooses not to annihilate Selma. She is mentioned in *The Undercurrent* and *The High Priestess,* though mostly for the sake of caricature. Not precisely one of Whitman's supermothers herself, she borrows a leaf from Aristophanes' *Lysistrata* in declaring that the American women will refuse to bear children unless the men swear off their destructive ways. Grant also informs his readers that as the wife of the American minister to Spain, she "aspired to put an end to bull-fights"—a grotesque aberration. How did she get to Spain instead of the White House? Horace Elton did get his revenge after all. [16]

There is justice even among corrupt people, so it seems, but one can take some positive comfort in another fact of life, its rapidity. Returning from Spain, Selma finds that she is out of date, a fate not unknown to some of today's feminists. Selma's climb is not the success of the true American dream. Hers is a perverted dream, reduced from the millennial hopes of a nation to the welfare of a short-changed group and even further to the advancement of one presumably slighted individual. In a true democracy, her insistence on the rights of the American people would be as questionable— since self-serving—as the alleged right of any group or individual to any exclusive privilege.

Summary. *Unleavened Bread* is not a masterpiece of the first order because its theme is not grand and complete enough, its characterization is not balanced enough, and its style is not natural enough. At the same time, it is Grant's best work because of its important social, political, and cultural message and its careful structure.

Selma White's ruling passion, her lust for power, is the book's basic theme. But Selma is not clear enough in her own mind about her needs and wants; her dreams of achievement remain vague: does she want to become a political force or a member of the social register or both? Frequently it appears as if she could be deflected from her populist course by a well-phrased and well-timed offer by the leading social group: if she were given the opportunity to join the enemy, she would not feel the need to beat her. Her lust for power stems from her failure to be accepted; there is nothing superhuman or demonic about her; she is basically not evil but only petty. Nor is her rise to power fully achieved; as a senator's wife she has a long way to go to the top, and even if she arrived there, she would not be able to command social acceptance and personal recognition by the aristocrats. In *The Undercurrent* and *The High Priestess,* Grant removes Selma—and with her the theme of power—to the periphery.

As Colonel Higginson pointed out to Grant, Selma is too starkly drawn, too one-dimensional. She has no humor; she never does anything good-natured; nor is she subject to the passion and suffering that save Emma Bovary from becoming a monster. Selma is cold and calculating; she invites dislike and fear only, not condemnation and sympathy alike. Finally, Grant's style—particularly as related to characterization—is all too often mechanical. Characters do not develop by action, do not gain contour and depth from within; they are presented as ready-made, and Grant's favorite stylistic methods are extensive authorial delineation and pat speeches from character to character rather than living dialogue.

Yet paradoxically, what on a high level of expectation must be counted as shortcomings can be regarded as strengths on a lesser level. Selma is one-dimensional, but that restriction sharpens the book's focus. One cringes at Selma's diction, but her stilted phraseology expresses her warped personality. And Grant does do some important things very well: Selma's tripartite rise from country girl to power figure gives the novel a clear and compelling progression; her combination of selfishness, ambition, provincialism, demagoguery, and ruthlessness creates a memorable portrait of someone who is definitely not a lady and who therefore must be checked if the fabric of American democracy is to be kept intact.

Unleavened Bread sold so well and was so well received that it was made into a play and caused Grant to consider resigning from the bench in order to give all his time to writing. The play, however, was only moderately successful, and Charles Scribner talked him out of becoming a full-time author, yet *Unleavened Bread* forever changed Grant's career as a writer from that of an entertaining amateur to that of a serious realist and satirist who discovered Main Street twenty years before Sinclair Lewis arrived on the scene.[17] Decisive as it is, *Unleavened Bread* did not exhaust Grant's probing of major social issues. Using its locale (the city of Benham), its chief character (Selma White), and—most importantly—its chief theme of the "new" woman, Grant added *The Undercurrent* (1904) and *The High Priestess* (1915) to complete a loosely connected trilogy which, in analogy to John Galsworthy's *Forsyte Saga,* may be termed the Benham novels.[18]

The Undercurrent

Unleavened Bread made its mark even with very busy and prominent readers. From the White House, President Theodore Roosevelt—a personal friend of Robert Grant's—pilloried the character of Selma White as representative of the most negative aspects of the feminist movement. Replying to one Amelia Glover, Roosevelt wrote:

I wish that you and she would read a novel called *Unleavened Bread,* by Robert Grant. The character of the heroine, Selma, especially in her sexual relations, is exactly and precisely such a character as produced by the writings and efforts of the woman whose newspaper letter you enclose, and whom you follow. This Selma represents her and your ideal of womanhood; and in all the ages there has been no more contemptible ideal.[19]

Pleased that Selma had made such a strong impression, Grant was also aware that "the success of *Unleavened Bread* had left me sensitive, nevertheless, to the imputation of being anti-feminist, if not a woman-hater, and I aspired to present a cross-section of the American scene in which woman should figure more admirably." He undertook to do so in his next novel *The Undercurrent* (1904).[20] The second in time of publication among the three novels that form Grant's composite picture of his contemporary America, *The Undercurrent* adds to the themes of Benham and the "new" woman a third, allying it with the later *The Bishop's Granddaughter* (1925): the ecclesiastical dimension of divorce and remarriage.

Orphaned Constance Forbes, a pretty, intelligent, and religious young woman, is on her way to Benham to become a schoolteacher when she is delayed by a train accident. During the wait, she becomes acquainted with Emil Stuart who then courts her for a year. When they marry, Constance realizes that they are a little young and that Emil is not perfect, but she is marrying for love and with open eyes. She has enough money to buy a little house. Emil is convinced that the phenomenal growth of Benham will enable any enterprising fellow to make his fortune within ten years. But he is rather an average man after all, and he is not religious, which hurts Constance, ruins their Sundays, and saddles her with the problem of "how to be true to her husband without being false to the church" (40). For a time, they enjoy a relatively happy family life, particularly when a boy and girl are born to them. But Emil is soon absorbed by his business enterprises; speculation, bankruptcy, and drinking mark his downward course. When he fails to win election to alderman, he vents his anger at Constance, whom he blames for supporting him too late and for not wanting to move to New York City to repair his fortunes after he first failed. Constance is shocked and forced to admit to herself that she has held an unrealistic view of her husband. Emil speculates with money not his own, is ruined once more, and decides to leave Benham for New York, deserting his family. His letter to Constance asserts at least that he still loves his children, and it no longer vilifies Constance, who in turn sends Emil a resigned letter informing him that she plans to keep the children.

Initial help comes from Mr. Prentiss, Constance's minister, who also introduces her to the wealthy Mrs. Randolph Wilson, a leader of the church and of civic, charitable, and aesthetic activities in

Benham. Mrs. Wilson will pay for Constance's training as a secretary; thus, Constance is able to use the equity from the sale of her
house to pay back the money Emil had misappropriated for his last
speculation and to begin her new life with a clean slate. Through
Mrs. Wilson, the reader is introduced to Benham's high society
with all its strengths and weaknesses. Miriam Wilson allies herself
with Mr. Prentiss who wishes to promote "American civilization
outside of church work" (91), believes in the church as "the beacon
of civilization" (99), and deprecates the "pleasure-loving, self-
indulgent, and purposeless leisure class" (105). Her brother Carleton
Howard is one of Benham's magnates, a hard-working, enterprising,
responsible capitalist, alive to the necessity of making money and
of spending it wisely for the betterment of mankind. His son Paul
is after his heart: good-looking, athletic, well-mannered, well-
educated, serious-minded, married, and ready to follow his father's
example. Mrs. Wilson's daughter Lucille is flightier in outlook, to
the point of marrying—much to Mr. Prentiss's consternation—a
worthless dandy from New York. Gordon Perry, a friend of Paul
Howard's, is a young attorney of personal and professional characteristics very similar to Paul's. Like Prentiss, Perry is bothered by
the contrast of rich and poor in the United States. Unlike Paul's
other friends, Perry does not believe in the "millionairium, an in-
genious American substitute for the millennium" (200). Through
Paul's intervention, Constance Stuart becomes Perry's clerk. Em-
ployer and employee like and respect each other; Constance also
makes a warm friend of Perry's mother who often babysits with little
Emil and Henrietta of her own accord.

   After further plot complications, Perry declares his love and proposes to Constance, who also loves him but cannot marry him
because a divorce from Emil Stuart to which she would be legally
entitled is against "the eternal fitness of things" (303). When Constance informs her of Perry's proposal, Mrs. Wilson replies: " 'A
blissful future is before you if you marry, welfare for your children
and yourself. But in the other scale of the balance are the eternal
verities, the duty one owes to society, the fealty one owes to Christ.
You spoke of beauty. The most beautiful life of all is that which
embraces renunciation for a great cause, even at the cost of the most

alluring human joys and privileges' " (341). After a similar session
with Mr. Prentiss, Constance renounces her possible happiness.
Perry's attempt to change Prentiss's attitude fails; their discussion
ends in a stalemate.

Mrs. Wilson elevates Constance to the position of her private
secretary. Both Perry and Paul Howard go into politics. Perry advances a "socialistic legacy tax bill" (452); when it is defeated,
Constance feels that she must be with him. In a final showdown
between the poles of society, Loretta Davis, a working class woman
who has been a figure in a subplot, assaults Mrs. Wilson in her
mansion after a grand ball. She accuses her of cheating even the
faithful Constance by urging her to give up Perry. Constance in-
tervenes to save Mrs. Wilson's life and to restore to her at least some
of the belief in beauty and the eternal verities which Loretta's attack
had badly shaken, but she also informs Mrs. Wilson that she has
decided, quite independently of this shocking occurrence, to accept
Gordon Perry after all.

Constance—as her name suggests throughout—does not act friv-
olously. She recognizes that by not marrying Gordon she would
commit a greater sin than violating the church position on divorce
could ever be. The outcome suggests that the approach of level-
headed undogmatic people like Gordon Perry and Carleton Howard
is preferable to and more effective and in the best sense more pro-
gressively American than the high exclusive ideal a few elite minds
like Mrs. Wilson and Mr. Prentiss cultivate. Although Mrs. Wilson
and Selma White are poles apart, the unproductive and potentially
destructive element in their quite different philosophies is a dangerous vagueness common to both, and both women are fond of the
tag "the eternal verities." In *Unleavened Bread,* Grant warns against
spread-eagle demagogy born of a lack and distrust of culture; in *The
Undercurrent* he cautions against an aestheticist theory of progress
and civilization derived from too great an insistence on culture and
tradition.[21]

The Question of Divorce. *The Undercurrent* is a weaker novel
than *Unleavened Bread.* To be sure, there is a wider variety of women
than in Selma's book, but the range from Mrs. Wilson to Loretta
(with Constance occupying the sensible middle ground) is more

confusing than convincing, since the plot somehow has to accommodate them all and manages to do so only at the price of being diffuse, sensational, and melodramatic. Worse yet, the characterization—except for Constance and Mrs. Wilson—is superficial, and even those two are easily recognized as a thematic pawn and a thematic mouthpiece. Grant was conscious of these weaknesses:

If instead of centring my interest on social problems, I had sought to create, at whatever cost, two or three other characters as original as Selma, I should have been a more enduring artist. From the novel-reader's point of view, a theme, however important, fades if the figures are not vital. I was aware of this when I selected the problem story which I finally called *The Undercurrent*; but because of my interest in social trends, I allowed myself to be engrossed by a theme before evolving the individuality of those to be affected by it. I was putting the cart before the horse; unconsciously, to be sure.[22]

The problem—the question of divorce—engaged Grant from *Unleavened Bread* on in novels, essays, and active attempts to bring about legislative changes in the divorce and marriage laws.[23] He knew that the problem was complex, that many feminist demands were justified, and that a new relationship between man and woman was inevitable. What he vigorously objected to was disorder, haste, excess. He did not like to see necessary reforms and adjustments drowned by a wave of sexual license and frivolous divorce which threatened to undermine the existence of the American family itself. He was the sort of progressive whose belief Richard Hofstadter analyzes in *The Age of Reform*:

The failures of American society were thus no token of the ultimate nature of man, of the human condition, much less the American condition; they were not to be accepted or merely modifed, but fought with the utmost strenuosity at every point. First reality must in its fullness be exposed, and then it must be made the subject of moral exhortation; and then, when individual citizens in sufficient numbers had stiffened in their determination to effect reform, something could be done.[24]

The great Progressive himself, Theodore Roosevelt, wrote to Robert Grant that he was taking a position similar to Grant's:

In the divorce matter, as you know, I come nearer to your position than I do to that of Mrs. Roosevelt. . . . It has been shocking to me to hear young girls about to get married calmly speculating on about how long it will be before they get divorces. It is mere foolishness for the woman like "Constance," who has been deeply wronged, to refuse to get a divorce and marry again. It is another thing to do as "the Four Hundred" does and show an atavistic return to the system of promiscuity.[25]

With *The Undercurrent,* Grant had wanted to write a novel "in which woman should figure more admirably." He succeeded insofar as Constance is indeed preferable to Selma, but he had not touched the heart of the divorce matter yet. Selma has her own way unreservedly; she does not live in partnership. Constance's situation is also essentially depersonalized: she is all good, Gordon Perry is all good, Emil Stuart is all bad. The focus in *The Undercurrent* is not on the relationship between man and woman but on the attitude of the church toward divorce. Grant needed to write a novel that studied the relationship between man and woman not obliquely but directly; he did so in the third Benham novel, *The High Priestess* (1915).[26]

The High Priestess

Because she wants to marry for love, Mary Arnold rejects wealthy Henry Ives Thornton and marries Oliver Randall, a fledgling lawyer who realizes that in marrying Mary "he had succeeded beyond his deserts" (31), that he is marrying "this high priestess" (32). Mary is a modern woman with new views of life and woman's role in it. Marriage is a partnership, allowing both man and wife to make the most of their individual abilities in a framework of mutual understanding. Mary herself is a talented decorator and plans to get ahead in her profession.

The Randalls' friends are the foil against which Mary's notion of a modern marriage develops (Oliver does not develop any notions of his own but cheerfully accepts Mary's ideas). Barbara Day has genuine literary talent, already considerable success in having her work published, and a most promising future. When Barbara marries Hamilton Ford, one of Oliver's friends, Mary is deeply upset: "Was it not deplorable that a brilliant woman's future should be sacrificed

to petty household duties which any ordinary person could perform?"
(6). To guard against a similar fate, Mary develops a domestic
program shorn of all superfluities and unnecessary creature comforts:
no useless furniture and articles, no heavy meals (to rise hungry
from the table would keep mind and spirit alert), no intoxicating
beverages. After a few months of marriage, "their common life ran
with the regularity and smoothness of a well-constructed mecha-
nism" (37). A constant example of the deleterious old-fashioned way
of doing things is given in George Patterson, Oliver's senior partner,
and his wife Nettie: she feeds him too much, she praises him too
much, she has no interests of her own, she likes partying. Another
friend of Mary's, Sybil Fielding, lives in Europe. A girl of sensibility
and artistic temperament, she should be embracing individual notions similar to Mary's. Instead, Mary concludes, "it looked as if
Sybil had accepted what was still, in spite of the Ibsen School, the
conventional continental theory of the relation between the sexes"
(10).

The Fords increase and multiply rather regularly, much to Mary's
annoyance. By contrast, her first child, a boy, arrives on schedule
and fills with gladness that part of her existence which she had set
aside for motherhood. She is happy, but there is only analysis in her
happiness, no spontaneity. Contrary to custom, she names the boy
after her own family, Martin Arnold, with the thought that the
"Martin" might be dropped by and by. Life continues as planned,
until "suddenly one day she was appalled to realize that she was
again to become a mother" (60). But Mary forces herself to accept
the inevitable and ultimately genuinely delights in the birth of her
daughter Mary Christabel. Meanwhile, the Fords have decided on
a revolutionary arrangement: in order to free the time and leisure
necessary for Barbara's rise to the top, Ham will do or oversee all
the housekeeping and raise the children. They get off to a good
start; Mary is delighted and sets to work again on her own life. She
receives a small inheritance and successfully urges Oliver to go into
business for himself. Soon, she wins first prize for a fountain design.
When Oliver returns from a trip with typhoid fever, Mary turns to
architecture in a serious way in order to keep the family going,
using her maiden name in her profession. She is in full control of

herself and decides "unreservedly that she was more than content not to have been born a man" (95).

Mary generally has some difficulty understanding men, including her own. She does not like his political friends and pours cold water on his political ambitions and enthusiasm. In a consummately executed scene, Mary forces herself to submit quite against her actual mood to Oliver's amorous desires. When, by chance, she reads a private letter he has received, she becomes aware that he has been helping a friend to rid himself of a woman in order to marry Sybil Fielding. Mary is shocked and tells Sybil, who breaks off the engagement, though for different reasons. Discussing this matter with Oliver, Mary discovers that they did not take "the same view of sexual irregularities" (105–06).

Grant accelerates what has been a very gradual process of drifting apart by an occurrence which at first sight might work out as well as the Fords' domestic arrangement: Mary hires Sybil as housekeeper. Oliver senses that he is losing Mary. Mary's talent is recognized and appreciated by professional architects; by contrast, Oliver's work finds a steady champion in Sybil. She takes an interest in his political activities, she begins to feed him food he likes and plenty of it, and she is always there; in fact, she sits in Mary's seat when Mary is absent, which as a rule she is. Mary's reputation and clientele increase; she is unhappy that she cannot become a full professional because Ollie is not like Ham, but once again she overcomes this feeling because her life plan has always taken account of her also wishing to be wife and mother. Mary is none of these to the fullest of her abilities but glories in the sense that she is all of these to a very satisfying degree after all.

When Ollie celebrates an important legal victory with a bottle of claret, Mary chastizes him for being "insubordinate in a connubial sense" (204). She tells him the full extent to which she will be leading her own professional life. He promises not to hamper her but has "the air of one showing the door to a familiar friend who had betrayed him" (210). Unhappy because she senses that Oliver, however proud he may have been of her recognition as a designer and architect, has never taken her seriously as a professional, she in turn commits the same error toward him. She happens to hear one of Ollie's political speeches and is astonished: "How happened it that he had become such a forceful, magnetic speaker without her knowledge?" (227). She attempts to rationalize, but "it remained true that he had certainly made of himself politically far more than she had supposed possible, and that she was immensely proud of him" (230). However, she does not tell him so, whereas Sybil gushes praise and admiration. Returning home from a party victory celebration a feted man, Oliver thinks over the contrast between Mary and Sybil: Mary is away, almost always; Sybil is there, always: "She would be waiting for him, eager to hear the full particulars, which he was looking forward to recount, and she undoubtedly would have some supper ready" (233). Mary sends a telegram, with no reference at all to the election: she is unavoidably detained. Sybil places the telegram in the book Mary has been reading, *The New Feminism*. Oliver briefly looks at the book but flings it away in disgust as "tommy-rot" when he reads: " 'There are signs that the day is not remote when man will not figure in the eye of a woman except as the father of her child.' " Meanwhile, "the sizzling eggs were ready" (239), prepared by Sybil. Inevitably, Oliver has nightmares over the situation, which results in his asking himself: "Which of these women was his wife and which did he prefer?" (246).

On Oliver's thirty-eighth birthday, Mary is once again away; Sybil, however, organizes a surprise party with sumptuous food and champagne. The occasion makes Oliver realize that he does desire Sybil and throws him back into the turmoil of conscience and inclination which he believed he had overcome. On the train home from New York, Mary revels once more in her new success. She thinks of herself as "a practical, living exemplar of the new womanhood which was replacing the old" (266) and fairly congratulates herself on having had the foresight to avoid the cold, sexless career attitude ascribed by male critics to that new order. She muses: "A sister for Christabel would be welcome now, if her advent might be timed to avoid conflict with any important piece of architectural work" (267). And it occurs to her "that hers was not the prayer for a man child—formula of a man-governed world—but rather the passionate hope that she might have a bevy of girls to share the golden opportunities of the next quarter century—the date to be known for all time as the Woman's Period—the day of complete equalization of the sexes, and the full recognition of the high place of woman in the scheme of race development" (267–68). Not only a repeated reference to a book on the issue titled *The Bee,* but Mary's entire train of thought and her feeling superior to Ollie, "her big, faithful mastiff" (271)—despite her efforts to see each other as equals—suggest that for the time being at least she very much enjoys the queen bee syndrome. Little does she realize the state of affairs at home.

Oliver has the opportunity to become a judge of the state court of appeals but is reluctant to go ahead because " 'on the bench—even the highest bench—I should be shelved' " (276). He appeals to Mary to make the decision for him; but Mary is unsure and refers the matter to Sybil almost automatically—though, as she realizes too late, certainly inappropriately. Secretly Mary favors Oliver's acceptance, but Sybil enlarges upon his doubts by appealing to Mary to oppose it. Taken aback by Sybil's fervor, Mary decides to check up on things generally. Running through the domestic accounts the next day, she makes a horrible discovery: "The offense which stood out, combining deceit with insubordination, was that Sybil, while following every rule punctiliously when under observation, had taken deliberate advantage of all her absences to introduce everything tabooed in the way of foods" (283). When she finds the champagne corks from the birthday party in the ashcan, she decides that Sybil has to leave. Oliver's refusal of the judgeship makes her wonder if there is anything between him and Sybil; she rejects the idea as unworthy of Oliver's proven trustworthiness and her own superior attractions but gladly takes advantage of another business engagement away from home to see what will happen during her absence. Returning unannounced, Mary comes upon a compromising scene between Oliver and Sybil who repulses him reluctantly because she is engaged to Henry Thornton, Mary's erstwhile admirer. Mary is crushed but moves quickly and relentlessly in declaring Oliver free and taking herself out of the house. Sybil tries to change Mary's mind but ultimately accuses her of having neglected and never really loved and appreciated Oliver: " 'You ridiculed his friends, you scorned his tastes, ignored his politics (his soul's vision) all in the name of your superior wisdom, and—like a man—he turned to me for consolation' " (304). Mary rejects the accusation—the proof of her love "lay in her aching heart" (307)—but circumstances would not matter anyhow: Oliver has been false to her, which is all that counts. Mary feels righteous, leaves the house, asks for help from the Fords, sends for the children, and refuses to accept any financial support for them from Oliver. Not seeking a divorce, which she recognizes as a stigma, Mary demands "something more vital and wide-embracing—the right to live reputably and bring up her children apart from her husband, because he had forced her to it, without the slightest loss of social prestige" (319). Yet she smarts from the knowledge that her marriage has failed.

Soon after the fracas, Sybil marries Henry Thornton. In due time, she has a baby, but the child is sickly and dies after a year. She is told that she can have no more children. During the years of Sybil's motherhood and subsequent despondency, many social changes take place. Her husband informs her that Oliver Randall is lieutenant-governor and in line for governor. In the meantime, Mary has prospered professionally. But when she becomes a candidate for president of the Woman's City Club, her marital circumstances come to the fore again and prove to be a disadvantage, although she does get elected. When Oliver becomes a candidate for governor, his son worries that his private life may be held against him; he urges Mary to make it up with Oliver. She refuses but divulges the entire story in order to kill Arnold's temptation to confuse ethics and expediency. Eighteen-year old Christabel is a disappointment to Mary. A pretty girl, she is not at all intellectual and rather "atavistic" (407) in her fondness for clothes and attentions by the other sex. Oliver is elected governor, and fewer and fewer of Mary's friends understand why she will not go back to him. She receives two significant honors and feels that she is holding her own. Still, she begins to take greater interest in Oliver's doings, wondering whether she had not underestimated him after all. When he passes up a chance to become a United States senator (his party is under attack for corruption, and although personally innocent, he refuses to take himself out of the firing line) and supports Henry Thornton instead, Mary is upset because she senses Sybil's influence. Entertaining high thoughts of a peaceful world run by women, Mary finds herself turning to local events once more when she reads in the paper that Henry Thornton is dead, Sybil a widow and free, and Oliver in dire trouble. Resenting the likelihood of Sybil's coming to Oliver's aid, she decides to help Oliver herself. Another development complicates her life: Christabel has become engaged to a Mr. Rivers and wishes to be married soon; unlike her mother, she has no desire whatever to be anything but a wife and mother. Though supportive of his daughter, Oliver feels sympathy for Mary for the pain Christabel causes her. Mary's sense of Sybil's doings has not been wrong: Sybil practically proposes to Oliver and forces him to see that he must either win Mary back or get a divorce if he hopes to have a happy life. Oliver writes to Mary for an appointment: " 'I must have either you or my liberty . . . your loving and contrite husband' " (487).

Mary makes good on her decision to rescue Oliver when she has a chance to steal and destroy the incriminating documents. She realizes that she has compromised her high standards, her notion that women are better than men, because of Sybil, of whom she is "fiercely jealous" (511). High priestess no more, she realizes that she has committed the same kind of accidental crime she has not forgiven Oliver for. This becomes paradoxically even clearer when she discovers that the papers she stole are only copies: Oliver also sins at one remove, as he never actually touches Sybil. The reader never finds out whether the real papers seal the ignominy of Governor Randall: the whole incident has served its purpose when it shows Mary that she too is open to temptation, be it for reasons far nobler than Oliver's infidelity. In a moving interview, she and Oliver even out their scores and begin life together once again, even though Mary helplessly cries because of the womanly lack of logic—the jealousy of Sybil—which rekindles her love.

A complex book, *The High Priestess* is as even-handed a treatment of the sexes as Grant was capable of. To be sure, he gives Mary Arnold many of Selma White's exasperating traits: the same neat, clear, crisp analytical bent; the same impersonal expressions; the same rhetorical questions; the same feminist intoxication born of wounded pride; the same pseudo-intellectual jargon rather than

words straight from the heart. But he makes Mary a fuller character
than Selma, ultimately less rigorous and therefore less memorable
but also less of a caricature. Mary *is* a cultured and talented woman,
she *is* a professional success of the first order, she *is* lovely, admirable,
and passionate. Most of all, what Mary learns is something Selma
never knows: if men fail, so do women, and mutual mercy is the
only answer. It is wrong to put woman on a pedestal and pretend
to revere her while actually taking advantage of her; it is equally
wrong to assume the position of high priestess, and perhaps Grant
should have given that title to Selma's, not Mary's, book.

Despite its fuller characterization of the heroine, *The High Priestess*
does not come up to the mark of *Unleavened Bread*. Its ambitious
theme—the discussion of a true partnership of man and woman—
is only partially carried through. Intellectually and temperamentally, Oliver is not Mary's equal; though a lawyer by profession,
he is not a very articulate advocate for man's cause. He is likeable,
but up to the point of becoming a captivating political orator, he
is little more than one of the boys: interested in food, sex, a good
cigar, an occasional night out, and otherwise peace and quiet. Mary,
by contrast, deemphasizes all creature comforts; her mind is a race-
horse in the hippodrome of the theory of marriage and the sexes.
Brooks Adams, who had had high praise for *Unleavened Bread*, was
very upset about *The High Priestess* and took Grant to task for a
reconciliation "where there is nothing to reconcile."[27] Once Mary
and Oliver separate, they seek out no companionship; it is hard to
believe that the full-blooded man and woman practice continence
for seven years. This unlikely behavior removes one of the most
serious problems in the long process of reconciliation and therefore
seriously undercuts the realism of the novel and the validity of its
theme.

Grant presents three different types of marriage: that of the Fords,
in which the traditional roles of husband and wife are reversed; that
of Sybil and Thornton, which is the traditional European model of
wifely submission; and that of Mary and Oliver, which eventually
ends in a desirably balanced partnership, in the new American marriage. In reality, only Sybil's and Mary's patterns are of importance:
they constitute the book's conflict. The Fords seem to be an excep-

tion, a quirk of nature almost; their pattern works because they happen to be the individuals they are, but Grant does not involve them in the central conflict in any meaningful way. Even the outcome of the conflict between Sybil and Mary is thinly motivated: not Mary's feminist notions—chastened by seven years of single life, loneliness, and reflection—carry the day but simple old-fashioned jealousy.

Finally, the novel does not have the technical merits of *Unleavened Bread*. It lacks that book's clear structure and progression. Many of the episodes are gratuitous; they neither advance the plot nor clarify the theme. *The High Priestess* is a full one hundred pages longer than *Unleavened Bread,* which at 431 pages is quite long enough. Incredibly, Grant "handed the manuscript over to a schoolteacher and critic of experience for professional revision of the phraseology. Because of the pressure of Court work, I might save time and receive valuable suggestions. The lady, almost a contemporary, proved zealous and thorough, but nearly every criticism was stamped with the preciseness of long ago."[28] The publishers were less than happy about this method of revision, and one does wonder about its effectiveness when one reads the kitchen diction of the book's opening sentence: "Mary Arnold's great happiness was made up of several ingredients" (1). Once again Grant had written a serious problem novel but not a great book.

Chapter Five
The Role of the Elite

Grant's views on marriage, divorce, and the "new" woman were not based on an uncritical and automatic adherence to convention. He kept his mind open, testing his belief against actual, current experience. Such experience came to him from his work as a judge and from his social life as an accepted member of Boston society.

In *Fourscore,* Grant writes: "I have no remembrance of having ever made literary use of an incident or situation arising in Court. While the human problems presented were constantly absorbing and sometimes perplexing, they were never subtle or dramatic from the point of view of literary reality."[1] And yet, while he could not make a literary character of the girl who asked him one day whether a woman could get a divorce from her husband because he smoked in bed, he felt forced to make literary use of the underlying trend. "As a Judge of a Court which saw the seamy side of matrimony, I must unconsciously have been influenced in my choice of literary subjects by what passed daily under my eyes, but more influenced by what I read between the lines and discerned on the horizon" (265).

Indiscriminate divorce and illicit sexual relations were not known in the society to which he belonged—and by way of his ancestry, his clubs, and his Harvard connections he was acquainted with just about everyone of social importance in Boston and Cambridge. That such matters were known to the rest of the country and especially the lower classes seemed of little importance to Brahmin Boston: "Sporadic, unsavory cases might induce a cock of the eye or shrug of the shoulders, but the ignorance of the mass as to how to behave was not a valid ground for substituting for well-mannered self-control ructions that were sure to pass" (259). Charles Eliot Norton, a distinguished Brahmin, urged Grant to ignore the themes of irregular sex relations and illicit love, but Grant was too disturbed by "the disintegrating attitudes at which the rest of the country was beginning to make sheeps' eyes" (259). If the leaders of society failed to take action, where would the necessary counterthrust come from?

With the exception of Mrs. Wilson and her brother Carleton Howard of *The Undercurrent,* no significant character in the Benham novels represents the American aristocracy. Howard's philosophy is merely stated rather than developed through action, and Mrs. Wilson's well-intentioned attempt to lead by making the nebulous eternal verities comprehensible and accessible through religious aestheticism fails to move not only the lower class (Loretta)—which could be expected—but also, disappointingly and despite some initial success, the middle class (Constance).

It had been Grant's contention in *A Romantic Young Lady* and *Face to Face* and several essays that the aristocrats—the truly rich, the leisure class—had the responsibility to lead America's unformed and uncertain democratic civilization in the right direction, a direction which would point ever upward physically, mentally, and spiritually through the twin forces of money and love united. He discusses the matter of standards and of leadership—the aristocratic leavening of the American democracy—in two quite different novels, placed between *The Undercurrent* and *The High Priestess*: *The Orchid* (1905) and *The Chippendales* (1909).

The Orchid

One of Grant's allies in the fight against the lowering of standards was President Theodore Roosevelt, who strongly disagreed with the negative tone discernible among certain members of high society.[2] Not only did New York's "Four Hundred" close their eyes as the Boston Brahmins did, some of them were actually guilty of setting negative examples. From Edith Wharton, Robert Grant heard "the report that a New York woman as one of the terms of divorce from her husband had sold her baby to him for two million dollars" (248). This report became the nucleus of his brief novel *The Orchid*.[3]

Lydia Arnold is a sophisticated, well-educated, introspective young woman, full of "opinions on many problems, sexual and otherwise" (4). She marries Herbert Maxwell because she thinks she might want to be married; besides, Maxwell is rich: his father made millions in the furniture business. Lydia is more interested in building a mansion and traveling than in her marriage. Soon, "Lydia's immediate plans met with interruption from an unexpected source" (63): she is pregnant. The baby is a girl whom she does not nurse and for whom she feels little affection. When fascinating Harry Spencer joins the exclusive colony of the Maxwells and their friends at Westfield, Lydia falls in love with him and realizes that she never loved Maxwell. She and Spencer meet frequently without actually committing adultery, until finally Maxwell calls her to account. She tells him that there are only two options: a European arrangement or a separation. Maxwell rejects the first but hands Lydia extraordinary leverage when he reacts very emotionally to her rather casual remark that she plans, of course, to take their two year-old daughter Guendolen. Lydia transforms this advantage into a divorce settlement which leaves her without admission of guilt and with two million dollars in exchange for her giving up Guendolen to Maxwell. This calculating and cold-blooded transaction is compounded by Lydia's insistence that she will marry Spencer and continue to live in the Westfield colony as though nothing shocking had happened: " 'If one has millions and good manners one can do anything in America; everything else is forgiven' " (181). She succeeds in averting Westfield's social ostracism, which was the only possible penalty that would have meant anything to her.

"Westfield" and "Arnold" provide specific connections with *Unleavened Bread* and *The High Priestess*. But Mary Arnold and Selma White are not aristocrats, and while Mary establishes a domestic regimen of a new kind, she is not interested in the gratification of an illicit sexual relationship. Neither is Selma, despite her potential for destructive leadership. If Lydia Arnold were a real lady in the sense of Flossy Williams's definition given for Selma's benefit in *Unleavened Bread,* she would at least be the equal of the well-meaning and cultured Mrs. Wilson of *The Undercurrent.* Instead, she is all negative and totally self-centered. She does nothing for anybody; even Spencer is essentially only the means to her personal happiness, as are Maxwell's millions. In Lydia, the union of money and love cannot become a force for the advancement of society because the love is of the wrong kind and the money too is ill-gotten: blood money, really, for the sale of what should be her most precious possession. Lydia's maxim is: one is what one is; Maxwell's: one is what one chooses to be. There is a frighteningly powerful and relentless logic in Lydia's unethical conduct, including her sharp calculation that everything—the love of a father and the social status within a community—has its price.

Grant catches the requisite social tone very well—a mixture of sophistication, indolence, and vapidity characteristic of the entire Westfield set. Like an orchid, Lydia is beautiful, parasitic, expensive; she too could not flower if she did not have the right growing conditions. Grant's real attack is against vacillating society, the "Four Hundred" (212) who ought to see themselves as patricians and moral leaders of the country but who are weak instead and in a moral sense venal. *The Orchid* does not have the complexity and texture of Grant's other divorce novels, but the rigor of its development makes it his most unsettling book of that group. It is a disturbing illustration of his contention that "marital infidelity has been the favorite excitement of every rotten aristocracy which the world has ever seen."[4] The message of *The Orchid* is harsh: the American aristocracy is in danger of going the way of all previous aristocracies.

The Chippendales

Shocking as the divorce settlement underlying *The Orchid* is, Grant was too much of a Brahmin to abandon all faith in the American aristocracy. He knew that his own society was not rotten, and he turned back to it for reassurance. In writing *The Chippendales,* "the long novel on Boston of the eighties,"[5] Grant "wished, while not extenuating the mordant popular gibe that its society was 'a state of mind,' or even 'the east wind made flesh,' to bring out certain characteristics essentially fine and sound at the core, though sometimes awkward, which gave that society distinction." It was to be a balanced book: "I was ambitious to give a true picture and perspective; to set in relief the high purpose and ethical aims of the New England conscience, and yet to write with my tongue in my cheek regarding the limitations among which I had been bred and of which I was consciously the victim."

A young man from Maine, whose father died in the Civil War and whose mother died shortly after his graduation from a small New England college, Hugh McDowell Blaisdell comes to Boston in the early 1880s with a letter of introduction to Horatio Langdon, the leading banker and his father's former brigadier. Blaisdell wants to succeed as a self-made man; his model is Abraham Lincoln (whom Grant had singled out as the apotheosis of Americanism in *The Art of Living*). But this early in the novel Grant emphasizes the importance of connections: however capable Blaisdell proves to be in his own right, it is the letter of introduction to Langdon which opens the door for Blaisdell. Langdon places him with a broker, and Blaisdell finds suitable lodgings at the house of Gideon Avery, an inventor who has a lovely daughter, Priscilla, and who has recently married an attractive widow from Ohio who also has a lovely daughter, Lora.

Priscilla is courted by a Boston blueblood, Henry Chippendale Sumner, whose father—like Blaisdell's—fell in the war. Stiff and principled, Sumner lacks enthusiasm and spontaneity: "In one of various efforts to persuade her that he was really a volcano in spite of appearances, he had watched at midnight the light of her bedroom window from the shadow of the Art Museum until she extinguished it—and told her so" (67). He is a very respectable scholar at Harvard, but Priscilla does not care for that kind of accomplishment. She admires Sumner's cousin Chauncey Chippendale, who distinguishes himself in football instead of Greek and is offered on the spot a position with Langdon. She also notices Blaisdell's common sense, energy, self-reliance, and swift progress. Priscilla wants to get married to be independent of her parents, but when Sumner proposes, she turns him down in a forceful scene in which she accuses him of being "the conventional, critical, cold type of Boston man which she abhorred" (104). When Blaisdell decides to court the less intellectual, doll-like Lora and easily wins her, Priscilla seems disappointed. But she does not need to stay in her father's house: she is offered and accepts a position as companion to the elderly though still vigorous and commanding Miss Georgiana Chippendale, Henry

Sumner's aunt, thus exposing herself to precisely the kind of people she wishes to move away from (" 'The Avery blood used to be deep blue, but the pigment has been diluted by years of close economy— low living and high thinking, Priscilla calls it' " [50]).

Leading representatives of the people who live on the water side of Beacon Street, of the Boston-Salem merchant aristocracy, the Chippendale clan includes Harrison, the titular head, his bachelor brother Baxter, and his sisters Georgiana and Eleanor, Henry's mother. Conservative Georgiana and Baxter live on Beacon Hill, whereas Harrison and Eleanor—going with the times—have moved to the Back Bay. Harrison has five children, among them Chauncey and Georgiana; Eleanor has two daughters in addition to Henry. Living as befits Chippendales—high-class but not extravagant— Harrison and Eleanor find that their incomes barely keep up with the mounting expenses necessary for the proper education and finishing of their children. They are relieved when Chauncey joins Langdon and when Henry sets up as a lawyer. Yet there is no denying the fact that it becomes increasingly difficult to continue their accustomed life-style. By contrast, Blaisdell soon understands everything about the stock market and becomes quite well-to-do. Refusing to speculate, Harrison decides to sell his mansion, which is bought by Blaisdell. Blaisdell embodies the new trend which Harrison cannot abide: "A man of this stamp, if not watched, is liable in time to undermine the whole social structure of Boston" (174).

Chauncey marries the boss's daughter, Beatrice Langdon. Priscilla becomes indispensable to Aunt Georgiana and earns the entire family's respect. In turn, her opinion of Henry Sumner becomes more favorable, although he continues to distinguish himself chiefly in upholding Boston's traditions, as when he agitates against a subway plan pushed by Blaisdell. Still as much in love with Priscilla as ever, Sumner confides to a friend that he cannot sacrifice his identity for love, that "the leopard can't change his spots" (219–20), only to be told to persevere, for perhaps the leopardess can change hers when she decides that her ideal of a partner does not exist. It is good advice. Suddenly wealthy because of her father's invention, Priscilla slowly but steadily becomes aware of the Boston heritage within

her. "Having declared her intention to settle down as a confirmed
Bostonian" (277), she still considers Sumner and herself to be in
opposite camps: he is the obstructive conservative, she the progressive traditionalist. Her true grievance is Sumner's attitude toward
her brother-in-law Blaisdell whom Sumner charges with "lowering
all our standards; of debauching public sentiment" (300). Challenged to give proof, Sumner agrees to do so as time goes on, but
what is really at issue is no longer Blaisdell's but Priscilla's character:
" 'If you do not see for yourself, I should not succeed in convincing
you' " (301).

An opportunity to see together soon occurs when a public debate
arises over the statue of a Bacchante, a gift to the Boston Public
Library. Admitting the statue's charm but considering it inappro-
priate for the central spot in the courtyard, Priscilla and Henry fight
side by side against Blaisdell and his followers. Priscilla discovers
"that the spur which was driving her on was the despised New
England conscience" (383). They win the fight, though Blaisdell
concedes only because his wife falls ill and dies. Priscilla offers to
take care of his children, now fourteen and twelve years of age. In
time, Blaisdell proposes to her, but she turns him down, though
without bitterness.

Meanwhile, Blaisdell's and Chauncey's business interests clash;
Blaisdell proves stronger and is determined to "annihilate" (495)
both Chauncey and Henry. He substantially accomplishes the first
by forcing Chauncey into admitting that he, Blaisdell, is the strongest. However, he decides that sheer destruction would be gratuitous:
he courts Chauncey's sister Georgiana instead, finally cracking the
irritating social barrier the Chippendale clan had erected around him
and his first wife. To finish Sumner, he must discredit him in
Priscilla's eyes. He attempts to do so by following Chauncey's chance
observation of Henry and Miss Brackett, Henry's secretary, who
seem to be engaged in a furtive tête-à-tête. It is true that Miss
Bracket is enamored of Henry, but when he does not requite her
passion she turns secretly to old Baxter Chippendale. Falsely sensing
a connection between Henry and Mabel Brackett, Blaisdell finds
himself in a situation very similar to Henry's vis-à-vis Priscilla: both
must bring proof for their accusations of the detested rival. Upon

Baxter's death, it is discovered that Miss Brackett is Baxter's wife and pregnant. She is still interested in Henry, and Blaisdell insinuates that Henry, not Baxter, is the father of her child. This gross behavior turns Priscilla against Blaisdell, who in turn is now ready "to declare that the grapes were sour" (535). Somewhat unhappily, Priscilla finds herself as opposite Blaisdell as she initially was opposite Sumner.

Further extraordinary events befall. Aunt Georgiana dies and leaves the bulk of her considerable fortune to Henry, on condition, however, that he drop the "Sumner" from his name. This is not as unworthy a condition as one might think, since it really expresses Georgiana's conviction that of the whole clan, Henry is the truest Chippendale. But Henry rejects it out of hand, to the amazement of the city and the sad but genuine admiration of his clan. He has always revered the memory of his father and could not possibly entertain what would be a dishonorable breach of filiality. Hardly past this hurdle, Henry decides to settle the last open question of his existence: he frankly confesses to Priscilla that despite three years' time he does not have any proofs against Blaisdell. In a beautifully and tactfully handled scene, Priscilla reveals that the leopardess has indeed changed her spots: " 'Don't go,' she said sweetly." For: " 'I found the proofs long ago.' " Stunned, Sumner is slow in grasping what is happening; lovingly, Priscilla chides his blue blood one more time: " 'Were you going to oblige me to offer myself to you, Henry?' " And she continues: " 'You are a typical Boston man; you have no real enthusiasm, no red blood; only an acute moral sense. And yet I love you. Think of that' " (579). She accepts him, and gladly so, because she has discovered and accepted her own New England conscience which she once suppressed and despised. " 'You have not really changed,' " she tells him, " 'but it's no matter—for I have tested you, my lord and master, and you are the truest of them all' " (580–81).

Sweet though their long overdue union is, it is Blaisdell who dominates the end of the novel. He joins the clan by marrying Chauncey's sister Georgiana, and Grant states flatly that "there are no more important people in Boston to-day than the Hugh Mc-Dowell Blaisdells" (598). Blaisdell has parlayed Electric Coke, Gideon Avery's invention, into "one of the great industrial corporations of the world" (600) and has Boston's single " 'first-class' fortune" (601). From Blaisdell's point of view, the old order is giving way to his new order, but Grant is not entirely convinced. For Blaisdell's marriage to Georgiana has given new strength to the clan: "Chauncey is a power down-town largely by reflected light, though the Chippendales are to-day, by virtue of their money and their connections, more signally than ever the leading family of Boston" (600). There is an innate tenacity of the old order whose direction one can perhaps influence and modify but which one cannot annihilate. To what degree does Blaisdell dominate the Chippendales, and to what degree have they coopted him? Grant hints that Blaisdell may have his comeuppance yet; or, at the very least, he leaves the matter open when he says of Boston: "Richer than ever in the fruits of its industry and thrift, seething—still seething—with all the problems of the universe, will it hold its distinction as a moulder of thought and a quickener of conscience when Henry and his like slumber with the mastodon and the buffalo? That is for posterity to answer. Or, if you are impatient to know, ask Blaisdell. He can tell you anything" (602).

Themes.   Unlike *Unleavened Bread, The Chippendales* is a balanced study of the clash between the old and the new. Grant avoids a nostalgic and doctrinaire defense of an order in which he himself was firmly rooted and in whose basic values he strongly believed. Once again the enlightened traditionalist rather than the immovable conservative, Grant realizes very well that society changes and—in America at least—rapidly so. Whether one welcomes the change is hardly the issue; Grant does not fight the inevitable but rather does his part to enrich the change with as much of the principles and accomplishments of the past as it will accept. Realizing that in America the new always gets the inside track, Grant wishes at least to give a fair account of what is too easily seen and rejected as old and worn out: he wishes to show that the past is not a dead weight but usable and living. In the context of Grant's ongoing reflections about the leadership role of the American aristocracy and its attitude toward marriage and divorce, his views of the relation between the sexes and of the relation between democratic and aristocratic viewpoints as expressed in *The Chippendales* are of particular importance.

Grant is aware—and critical—of woman's increased material expectations. Morgan Drake, an unsuccessful novelist, and Professor Patton discuss the subject in a half-serious, half-humorous fashion over lunch at the Sphinx Club, concluding that neither of them is modern and energetic enough to be of much interest to women: "The hero of the modern mating girl is the man who does deeds which can be measured in dollars and cents" (209). Drake and Patton—and of course Henry Sumner—do not do such deeds: they are the futile though noble upholders of an intellectual Boston which is on the wane. Later on, Chauncey Chippendale and Beatrice Langdon—whose engagement had prompted the discussion at the Sphinx Club—clearly illustrate Drake's point. Chauncey cannot afford to give his wife a new pearl necklace for Christmas because business sense dictates that he buy as many shares of Electric Coke as possible. His wife is unhappy but willing to postpone the purchase: "She had inherited the Boston tradition that it was fundamentally wrong to buy anything for which one could not pay from one's income, but she cherished as a corollary to this the expectation that her husband's income would be large enough to provide her with everything she desired." Chauncey too is unhappy: "He had the American husband's dislike of refusing anything to the woman for whom he was educated to slave" (340).

Democracy comes in for even more severe criticism. Drake and Patton consider "whether democracy is not making a mess of things" (211); they despise "the latest world-movement—the march of the common herd" (212) but realize that they cannot effectively oppose it. Henry Sumner is keenly aware of his problem, which is how "to become a force in this easy-going democratic Boston" (308). Discussing the local mayoral election, in which he will soon become an independent citizens' candidate, Sumner is relieved when Priscilla herself supplies the characterizations of democracy uppermost in his mind: " 'Democracy's constant peril seems to be that it idealizes second-rate people and standards' " (490), and: " 'You mean that our democracy is self-complacent?' " (491). These assessments are important inasmuch as Priscilla applies them as criteria for judging

Henry Sumner on the one hand and Blaisdell on the other. Judged by the aristocratic standard, Blaisdell is found wanting, exemplarily so in the crucial scene at Baxter's home where he insinuates an illegitimate relation between Sumner and Baxter's wife. Although Baxter's marriage is odd by its secrecy, Baxter's age, and Mabel's social status, it is not an indication of loose morals on the part of Baxter but simply of his unorthodox individualism, and the Chippendales and Sumners do not feel that anything needs to be hushed up.[6] Blaisdell, however, makes the sexual innuendo, and it is Priscilla who links sex and democracy in her view of Blaisdell: "He stood revealed to her at last in all the urbane complacency of a spiritual opportunist whose plausible vitality was constantly employed in obliterating the landmarks of the soul. With a discerning shudder, she shrank enlightened from the easy-going democratic philosophy whose conception of excellence was to raze every mountain peak to the level of the plain with no more concern than it removed any other obstacle in order to erect a new apartment house" (523).

That Priscilla's judgment of Blaisdell is made in architectural and environmental terms makes it almost a foreshadowing of modern America's suburban growth and urban plight and their underlying causes, but objectively her judgment is too one-dimensional. Grant himself knew very well that it was people like his ancestor Mason who leveled the original peaks of Beacon Hill, and that democracy cannot be reduced merely to a question of standards and complacency; although he was just as much a champion of excellence as his major old-style Bostonian characters, he makes it obvious that Blaisdell, in his own way, is rather first-rate too: an apparent conflict which Grant manages to defuse at least partly when Blaisdell marries a Chippendale.

Grant gave *The Knave of Hearts* the subtitle "a fairy story," which it does not deserve. But in *The Chippendales,* as in *Unleavened Bread,* fairy-tale elements and references abound. Blaisdell's early history as an orphan and his coming to Boston to seek his fortune are pure fairy-tale motifs, as is his splendid success, although his life does not conform to the rigid ethical requirements of a fairy-tale hero. Henry's wooing of Priscilla appears to Lora "a good deal like the case of the Prince in the fairy tale and Cinderella" (48). Lora sees her own social rise and desires in terms of the tale of the fisherman and his wife; the recollection helps her overcome a disappointment but also convinces her that her wish for a suitable house in the fashionable part of Boston is by and large justified and certainly in line with the proven assets of her fish—after all, she does not reach for the sun and the moon, that is, for being the wife of the president of the United States. Henry too resorts to a fairy tale analogy to express his feelings for his rival: "As a social factor Blaisdell was the antipodes of himself—the prosperous ogre to whom he yearned to play a Jack the giant-killer" (298–99). Henry's ultimate winning of Priscilla is his reward for a task fulfilled: she specifically tells him that he has passed her test, thus giving the Cinderella story an appropriate twist.

Characters. In *Fourscore,* an amused Robert Grant relates that Boston society was convinced that *The Chippendales* was a *roman à clef,* and that one clergyman "was able to supply the true name of every character in the book" (291). This is surely a tribute to the force and authenticity with which Grant depicted his characters, for he emphasizes in his autobiography that "I scrupulously avoided personalities in writing *The Chippendales.* All of its characters, however individual, were types; not one was copied from life. This was true also of the incidents except the controversy over the figure of the Bacchante."[7] Yet some of the types do have traits of Grant himself or members of his family, and some events and institutions seem taken from his personal experience. Grant was a club man, and the Tavern Club appears as the Sphinx Club in the novel.[8] Grant himself held civic positions Harrison Chippendale also held: overseer of Harvard and others. *Fourscore* contains a photograph of a "Fancy Dress Party, 1876," with Robert Grant and his sister Flora dressed in oriental costumes reminiscent of the garbs Henry Sumner and Priscilla Avery wore at their dress party. Grant took considerable pride in the prowess of his brother Henry and especially of his own son Patrick on the Harvard football team, so that Chauncey Chippendale's heroics appear familiar. Finally, Grant admits to a strong affinity with Henry Sumner: "I recognized enough of myself in him to be able to depict him exactly as he was, even when prevented by unworthiness from following him. Would I have refused to change my name to Henry Chippendale and drop the Sumner in order to inherit a fortune? Not when I wrote the book. Yet I almost liked to believe that I would have when Henry Chippendale Sumner's age." But all these parallels and autobiographical touches do not suffice to make any character or incident a key. Other Boston sons played football at Harvard, agitated against the Bacchante, went to costume parties, and were club members. For all the characters, Grant could claim what he does for Henry Sumner: "My description of his personality, if not wholly applicable to myself, corresponded to that of the scions of many families I could have mentioned."

The Best Woman. In Grant's novels from *Unleavened Bread* to *The High Priestess,* the quality of a woman is directly proportional to her view of marriage and divorce. Constance Forbes of *The Undercurrent* is somewhat outside this scheme, since she is essentially an innocent victim of the unprincipled Emil Stuart and the unbending doctrine of the church. The other four, however, are all free agents. Least worthy is Lydia Arnold of *The Orchid*: she is a selfish, greedy monster who acknowledges no principle but that of total self-gratification. She is particularly detestable not only because she hurts a decent man and sells her child, but because she is a member of the aristocracy, of the social elite supposed to set positive examples. Selma White, once divorced and three times married, is next in line. She is not as culpable as Lydia Arnold because she is not of the aristocracy and because her insatiable thirst for power and recognition, though narcissistic, is not cold-bloodedly selfish: Selma is not conscious of a desire to gratify herself only; she really believes that she wants to do "things" for the benefit of the American people and the human race. Selma is blind and destructive but not inherently evil.

Mary Arnold of *The High Priestess* comes next. Like Lydia, she is well-educated, aesthetic, and highly sensitive. Unlike Lydia, she is neither frivolous nor without a positive purpose in life: she wants to combine a happy, full-blooded marriage with her aspirations to become a designer and architect. In that sense, too, she has a more fully and clearly defined view of life than Selma, from whom she also differs in her almost total lack of spiritual parochialism. Too intent on her development as a new—that is, independent—woman, she neglects her husband, whose unfulfilled needs then set up the scene which leads to the separation. It is Mary who insists on that separation, even though Oliver and their friends urge her not to do so. But Mary redeems herself through her subsequent behavior, which makes the separation turn into a reconciliation rather than a divorce.

The best of them all, however, is Priscilla Avery of *The Chippendales.* She wants to marry to become independent of her parents, but she does not want to marry at all costs. Rather than stumble into a hasty marriage with Henry Sumner or accept Blaisdell's offer of marriage after Lora's death, she would rather remain an old maid than take a chance. There is enough of the "new" woman in her: she makes up her mind for herself, and she supports herself when she has to. But unlike Mary Arnold, she does not make marriage a testing-ground for independence; she solves her problems before she gets married, thus sparing herself and her husband and children the sorrow Mary, Oliver, and their children experience. Like Mary, Priscilla is a full-blooded woman, attractive alike to such different men as Sumner and Blaisdell. This is what she looks like just before Blaisdell proposes to her: "A sea breeze drawing across the lawn lightly stirred the wealth of wavy dark-brown hair which rose from her broad fair brow. She looked, as she stood there, revealing her full stature, the embodiment of entrancing, intelligent womanhood, ripe for the arms of a lover" (449–50). Though Grant found the model for at least the personal appearance of Priscilla in his wife Amy, he reached all the way back to earliest Puritan times for Priscilla's name and even some aspects of her courtship by Sumner: his Priscilla is a younger sister of "the Puritan maiden Priscilla" who was courted by the stout Captain Miles Standish but won by the tongue-tied John Alden.[9]

If Grant's idea of womanhood, then, is "full of the name and the fame of the Puritan maiden Priscilla," his Priscilla Avery is also strikingly close to the girl whom William Wasserstrom sees as the embodiment of gentility's "private and distinguished understanding of the connections among idealism, sex, love, and civilization—the supreme achievement of the genteel tradition."[10] Like Priscilla Avery, Robert Grant the novelist comes home in *The Chippendales*. Not Benham or Westfield or New York but Boston knows the way now as it always has. The aristocrats are not put to the test in the early novel *A Romantic Young Lady,* and only tentatively so in *Face to Face*; they fail mildly in *The Undercurrent* and miserably in *The Orchid*. But *The Chippendales*—without falsifying the historical fact of the decline of the old order—sees them tested and pass the test. Standards need not be abandoned if the right leadership is present and if compromise means the gradual cooption and elevation of the newcomers. *The Chippendales* is not only Grant's finest novel next to *Unleavened Bread* but also, because of its note of hope, his most positively American.

Chapter Six

Shell-shocked: World War I and Its Aftermath

The years between *The Chippendales* (1909) and *The High Priestess* (1915) were busy ones for Grant, so busy in fact that he did not have time for a careful personal revision of the latter novel. The Probate Court was no longer a place where old women might tell their woes; it had been "made over to meet the requirements of the foreign-born and an industrial era."[1] The workload increased steadily, and Grant found less and less free time for writing after ten years as a judge: "So steady had the work of the Court plus my avocations become by the end of 1903 that by Saturday noon I was always tired" (239). Although much of the court's business was mundane and repetitious, Grant found it satisfying on the whole: "The sessions where only contested cases were heard provided a succession of problems arising from new statutes and new theories of social justice, on the correct solution of which human welfare depended. Even the most sordid of these called for sympathy and understanding" (312).

Grant's avocations were not just club life, the theater, Brahmin social life, golfing, and fishing. He was increasingly in demand at Harvard, primarily as a member of its Board of Overseers. An exciting event was Theodore Roosevelt's visit to Harvard in February 1912 for a club dinner and an Overseers' meeting; Roosevelt stayed at the Grants' home on Bay State Road and turned it into political headquarters, formulating his plans to run for a third term as president, although he had to do so against his own party and former protégé Taft (who was also a good acquaintance of the Grants).

During these years too, Grant's sons had grown up; three of them had graduated and married by the time World War I broke out.

Robert, the eldest, lived in London as the American representative of the Boston law firm of Lee and Higginson. Always avid travelers, the Grants now had a ready-made reason for summer trips to England and the Continent "at least every other year" (305).

The War

Whether the hopeful spirit of *The Chippendales* is the opinion of a philosopher or the conviction of a grandfather is difficult to decide. Certainly it was shaken by the American attitude toward World War I. Finding fiction at a time of supreme crisis "a puppet show," Robert Grant turned his literary efforts to propaganda and wrote poems and essays in the cause of helping the Allies. Even more active was Amy Grant, who received two high decorations by the French government for her relief work. True to his basic philosophy, Grant did not object to "Germany's ambition for a place in the sun, but her ruthlessness and disdain for good faith stuck in my throat."[2]

Grant's war poems have no great literary merit, but they show spirit and commitment to what is almost a religious cause.[3] "The Superman" attacks "the insatiate Teuton pride" and brands the "Prussian power" as the Anti-Christ threatening the world. "The Loyal Legion" is a humorous poem on the Irish Legion which was expected to fight for Germany but by way of a drinking spree rediscovered in time its loyalty to Britain. "A Message" was published alongside the contributions of illustrious authors in Edith Wharton's *The Book of the Homeless;* it celebrates Belgium and is critical of America's neutrality. Finally, "A Hymn" rejoices in the long awaited entry of the United States into the war.

Visiting England and—through the intervention of Edith Wharton—the trenches near Rheims in France in 1916, Grant wrote down his observations and published them as *Their Spirit: Some Impressions of the English and French During the Summer of 1916.*[4] The Grants had visited England in 1914; now, at the height of the war, they went there again, partly to visit their son and his family, partly to get "as near as possible to the most terrific thing that has ever happened" (1). Except for his observations on the combat zone, Grant reports on "everyday and unspectacular conditions" (preface), but the cumulative force of the quiet and heroic determination of the French and the English to win this war for civilization's sake is evident on every page. As an involved American, Grant reports sadly that the Allies are disappointed by America's attitude. His chapters, originally published in the *Boston Evening Transcript,* are therefore essentially exhortations to the American people and the American government to join so righteous and vital a cause. His fervor is so genuine that the impressionistic, loosely organized pieces and the often pathetically trite metaphors weaken the rousing effect of his mission only slightly:

> Nevertheless the attitude of our rank and file in this crisis, of whose sentiments our President [Woodrow Wilson] is believed to be the mouth-piece, has given fresh life to the old European suspicion that the United States loves high-sounding phrases, but will side-step at a pinch, and has caused both the English and the French to feel that by failing to rise above the height of the dollar mark and its own immediate safety, the foremost exponent of aspiring democracy has missed the grandest opportunity to protest against wrong ever offered to a nation. (42–43)

America of course redeemed herself by joining the war in 1917, and it is therefore not the question of her international reputation which dominates Grant's subsequent writings but the war's reverberations on the American social scene.

The Crusade Against Indiscriminate Divorce

Grant's worries about the more excessive demands promulgated by the woman's emancipation movement were intensified by the war and its effect on American civilization. He was particularly upset about the dramatically increasing sexual libertinage he had so forcefully condemned in *The Orchid.* First in a number of essays and then in two novels he pointed out the destructive potential of woman's new self-centered attitude and agitated against what he considered a perverted view of progress with all the force of his convictions and his satirical wit.

Law and the Family. Law and the Family is a collection of papers Grant wrote between 1916 and 1919.[5] Except for two which deal with wills and estates ("The Third Generation and Invested Property" and "Perils of Will-Making"), these papers concern them-

selves less with the law as it affects the family than with the burning
contemporary problem of woman's liberation. The law, as Grant
points out, generally lags behind the course of social change, and
it is primarily to his professional experience of this situation that
the essays are due. For Grant here speaks as judge of the probate
court as which the title page of the collection identifies him. Yet
much of his view is familiar from *The Orchid* and the Benham novels,
and much of it will recur in *The Bishop's Granddaughter* and *The
Dark Horse.*

It is a man's view, an informed, enlightened, understanding view,
but a man's, and a judge's to boot. "Woman and Property" points
out that woman's rights in this area are significant at the time of
writing, whereas they were practically nonexistent in the olden days:
woman should reflect on the progress already made. With a little
more interest, coaching, and experience, she should be perfectly
capable of taking care of her own property and of administering that
of others. Grant readily concedes that she possesses or may acquire
the managerial skills—to borrow a modern phrase typically found
with reference to balancing one's checking account—necessary for
the clarification of her business life. Yet ultimately the problem is
not one of woman's greater knowledge but one of changed attitude:
Grant suggests that as she learns about managing money and property, woman ought to become less financially demanding on man,
less wasteful. The basic issue is not whether or not woman should
become economically independent but how soon she will give her
hardworking husband a break. Pointedly, Grant insists that the
European wife helps to save and build a man's wealth, whereas the
American wife spends it.

"Feminism in Fiction and Real Life" shows a similar pattern.
Grant concedes a vital point: "Woman has suffered so much in the
past from oppression that it is not unnatural she should think of
herself as still oppressed" (120–21). But he is quick to point out
that with the exception of the ballot the American woman at that
time is not lacking in any right the American man enjoys, and that
in addition "she is indulged as no other women in the world have
ever been" (124). There is no mention of equal pay for equal work,
affirmative action, and other employment issues of today. Rather,

woman's cry of inequality is seen as not so much legal as social, and what she particularly has "in mind involves the sex relation" (136). That is, what woman really rebels against is her tying herself to one man for life, against the notion that she may not ever without reproach or stigma seek greener pastures. Helpless before this urge, Grant wonders whether "the sophisticated woman of our day knows too much for her own happiness" (147). What he finds hard to swallow is the underlying demand of woman that she may fully decide for herself, and that this power include the right to err and to inflict harm on others—just as man does. Appealing to woman's older and nobler instincts of suffering and self-sacrifice, Grant cites the war years as an example of woman's true capability, and he comes within an inch of denouncing "certain leaders" (162) of the movement as demagogues.

Quite naturally, such considerations lead into a discussion of "Domestic Relations and the Child," "The Limits of Feminine Independence," and "Marriage and Divorce." Grant here rehearses all the facts and arguments which have with hardly a change survived the better part of the twentieth century: that man and woman *are* different, that therefore their social functions differ, that custody and divorce laws favor woman, that woman has the power to uphold or destroy the family unit, and that ultimately the danger lies not in the just redress woman is demanding for past and present wrongs but in her expecting too much, her urge for overcompensation. Even Grant's hobbyhorse, a uniform marriage and divorce law, will do little good if the general attitude of society is not sane and reasonable. And once again Grant looks to Europe: "People in Europe still expect to stay married even though disillusioned and are correspondingly circumspect in consenting to wed" (257). Perhaps, he suggests, the fault lies with democracy, which substitutes the painless, easygoing, mediocre way of doing things for pain and principles and standards.

Toward a Federal Uniform Marriage and Divorce Law.
Then as now, not all women wished to follow the liberation movement. Deeply disturbed and offended by the widely varying states' laws and "the hypocritical use of temporary residence in an easygoing State for the purposes of divorce," Grant spoke, wrote, and

testified for a uniform federal law, joining forces with legislators and conservative women's organizations. "A Call to a New Crusade" is a forceful statement of his position, concluding with a call for action: "It is with the hope of stimulating the patriotic women of the nation to band themselves together in defense of the family, their most precious concern, that this article is written. What are you going to do about it?" Similar pieces appeared in the *Pictorial Review* and the prestigious *Yale Review*. If their tone is forceful and preachy, it is so partly because Grant had realized that the gentle style of most of the Fred-and-Josephine essays was hopelessly outdated.[6]

Because of the "disaffection for all projected amendments to the Constitution of the United States induced by the widespread repugnance to the National Prohibition Law," Grant decided that he "was championing a losing cause," and that "the only possibility of fixing public attention on the hypocrisy and subterfuge incident to the flood tide of divorce seemed to be in laughing it out of Court." To that end, he wrote *The Bishop's Granddaughter* (1925).[7]

The Bishop's Granddaughter

Placed between *The High Priestess* (1915) and *The Dark Horse* (1931), *The Bishop's Granddaughter* is Grant's only novel of the twenties. Next to *Unleavened Bread*, it drew the warmest response from Grant's literary friends. Edith Wharton thought it his "best novel since *Unleavened Bread*," Owen Wister called it "the best job you've done yet," and Gamaliel Bradford built upon it an assessment which Grant proudly echoed later in self-characterizations: "What does appeal to me is your delightful Aristophanic skill in applying the comic principle to American life." Grant's secret, according to Bradford, is his ability to "somehow manage to keep up with young America."[8]

Following previous examples of his own (especially *Face to Face*) but most clearly those of Henry James's international novels, Grant creates as the central figure of the book a sympathetic foreign observer, three fifths of whose family have become American through marriage. Alfred John Barnegate Fortescue, bishop of Stotesbury, is a hearty sexagenarian, "a live man still in his prime" (2), who finally manages to make his long-postponed visit from England to the United States to visit his family there, especially his granddaughter Angela, whose baby he has been invited to baptize. A high churchman, the bishop is ethically a Mid-Victorian, yet he prides himself on always having turned his face to the future. He is aware that the Great War has temporarily (so he believes) dislodged certain basic societal assumptions and customs on both sides of the Atlantic, but he is convinced that presently the shell-shock will wear off and life return to the stable foundations upon which Western civilization is built, chief of which is the cohesive unit of the family, the holiness of matrimony. He knows very little about America and is initially rather inclined to accuse all Americans of Daisy Millerism, but his American companions on board ship manage to awaken his full interest in the American paradox of a nation highly idealistic yet at the same time most practical: what interests the bishop "most deeply" is "the true psychology of the nation he was on the way to visit" (33). This thought quickly takes on a sharper focus as the bishop learns that divorce is "the obvious, the outstanding 'ideal' the American people are united in pursuit of" (46). The bishop begins to understand that shell-shock will no longer do for an explanation, and that the concept of family is being redefined in America not in a clandestine apologetic manner but in an open and essentially political debate which postulates individual freedom and happiness as a constitutional ideal if not a constitutional right. Predictably, the bishop is not ready to concede that the holiness of matrimony should be subject to the supreme democratic virtue of total individual gratification; indeed, he hopes to do his part in curing the aberration by tentatively agreeing to write—for a princely fee—an antidivorce article for *Hearth and Home,* a leading American family magazine with an enormous circulation: "The 'American Scene' (he remembered the phrase as Henry James's) had resolved itself for him into an intensive study of the institution of marriage illumined by the hope of being able to convince an errant American public that, if wedlock ceased to be thought holy, social chaos could not fail to result" (81).

With extraordinary structural deftness, Grant makes the bishop's American experience an inexorable series of disquieting moral discoveries sharply set against the country's physical "tonic quality" (113) and his longing for peace and love. His great-grandson will be named for him (all four names), but will he grow up in the ancestral virtues? Grant combines psychological with topographic progression: slowly but steadily the bishop works his way to a heart-to-heart talk with his granddaughter, but much distance must first be traversed even after the transatlantic voyage. The car ride from the pier in New York City to the family estate on Long Island is a physical and cultural exploration at the end of which the bishop obtains his first glimpse of Angela:

The little brown velvet cap pressed down upon her head, her deep white collar with its parti-colored hem, her narrow yet unimpeding skirt,—the carefree costume suited her girlish figure admirably. Yet in this guise she might almost have stepped out of a canvas of the renaissance, a winsome page if not a noble lady. The art to conceal art. The Bishop knew himself apt at such a discovery. Yet what did her freedom presage except innocence and faithfulness? His eyes filled with tears. It was a precious moment. He was bringing holy church to his beloved exiles, from whom after this ceremony of religion and love he would cease to be estranged. (118)

But the bishop's love and good will are put to a severe test. Before long he discovers that the marriage between Willard Hood and Angela "still lacked perfect adjustment" (127). But only that, and the baptismal ceremony itself appears to the bishop the best confirmation that Angela and her social circle are a living reproof of the disintegration of the old family virtues. Yet again, the feeling is deceptive. He is told that nearly ten percent of the guests are or were divorced. One woman in particular, twice divorced and three times married, arouses his anger, although Grant's handling of the scene makes clear on the one hand that the bishop would rather not pay too much attention to her who he thinks is obviously an unusual case, a misfit, and on the other that her case is not at all unusual, that she does not stand out but blends in: "If discernible at all, she was but a speck among the loitering figures" (166). Far more disconcerting is the discovery that the baby's godmother, Rebecca Hyatt, is thinking about a divorce. She, whose face the bishop declares to be the "American face" (154), is purposely kept away from his company at the reception, and even his vigorous attempt—tinged, ironically, by latent eroticism—to catch up with her before she drives away fails. Thus, the book moves closer and closer to its shattering center: from the quiet theoretical discussions on board ship to rather atmospheric interferences to the thrice-married Mrs. Berwin to little Barney's godmother to Angela: from the ocean to New York to Long Island to the estate's public portions (the dining hall, the pergola, the sweeping lawns) to the privacy of the bishop's room upstairs.

The passage of time too conforms to this pattern: the leisurely ocean voyage turns into a brisk kaleidoscopic car ride, the days at the estate turn into a tumultuous rush of events on the day of the baptism. For it is after Mrs. Hyatt's departure and before the dinner hour that Angela seeks out her grandfather to tell him: " 'It's Willard and me of course' " (211). She believes, in the words of a journalist friend, that divorce is "really democracy's moral safety valve" (190) and forces the bishop against the wall: " 'I'm trying to find out, if you can tell me, what really good reason there is for sticking when one knows one's a misfit and could like someone else better if one had the chance' " (216). The American scene resolves itself into an intensely personal problem for the bishop who has lost all interest in setting the errant American public right if only he can prevent disaster in his own family. Yet he does not have a good reason to give Angela which has not been "shot to pieces long ago" (237). What ultimately gives Angela pause is her grandfather's realization that " 'Yes, men must do better, appreciably better' " (231)—a hint not lost on Willard, who proceeds to do something and begins a career as a movie star—and the sheer force rather than logic of his convictions: " 'Does the pursuit of your own poor individual happiness, at the expense of all law and decency and to the eternal detriment of holy matrimony, appear to you a noble ideal for an American woman—for any woman?' " (218) So Angela and Willard decide, however tenuously, to stick it out after all, and a crusty rich aunt manages to persuade Rebecca Hyatt to do likewise.

The bishop does write his article and has, all in all, a pleasant homeward voyage, but he continues to be worried by the narrow escape and the general import of his experience: "His family had escaped, but what of the great idealizing Republic? His mind would never wish to be free from the incubus of the wonder—will the United States bend its mighty democratic energies to combat this disgraceful orgy, or will the poison burst its boundaries, infecting the civilized world, and divorce on the ground of boredom become the best of reasons?" (280) In fact, precisely because he was spared does he refuse to "let the United States go hang" (235) when his American daughter-in-law who lives in England tells him that his article will not advance the Uniform Marriage and Divorce Law but that " 'it was noble of you to do it, anyway, and it shows us up fast enough as a law-evading, hypocritical lot' ": " 'You're wrong, my dear, I'm positive. They won't let it continue. I have implicit faith in the idealism of the American people,' " he answers, only to catch himself with a Jamesian suspicion: " 'God bless my soul,' he thought to himself. 'Have I, too, become contaminated?' " (298)

Not Selma White, not Mary Arnold, only the composite true Bostonian of *The Chippendales* matches the force and color of the character of Alfred John Barnegate Fortescue. Grant's tone is both incisive and mellow but above all gives evidence of a finely tuned human understanding. In no other novel of his do character and theme work so well together with—to use Henry James's famous phrase—"solidity of specification."[9] *The Bishop's Granddaughter* is a gentle and wise book; it is Grant's masterpiece of characterization and style, and not quite the equal of *Unleavened Bread* and *The Chippendales* only because of its narrower thematic focus.

The Dark Horse

Grant, his friends, and some discerning reviewers did laugh "the laughter of the gods," but the issue of "the hypocrisy and subterfuge incident to the flood tide of divorce" stayed in court. As the bishop returns to England, so Grant returns to Boston as he had done once before in *The Chippendales*. Subtitled "A Story of the Younger Chippendales," *The Dark Horse* (1931) marks Grant's retreat to Beacon Hill to see how the clan has survived the Great War and the Roaring Twenties.[10]

Chapter 1, "The Prologue to a Tale," briefly recounts the essentials of *The Chippendales* from the point of view of Harrison Chippendale, the head of the family, mellowed by the wise and humorous perspective of age—for Harrison Chippendale, long-lived like the family in general (another indication of the tenacity of the old order), dies in 1912 at the ripe age of eighty-eight. Although the Chippendale clan was briefly threatened with annihilation by the newcomer Hugh McDowell Blaisdell, it avoided defeat by coopting the shrewd, energetic Blaisdell through marriage with Georgiana, Harrison's daughter. Surveying the state of affairs, Harrison can reflect shortly before his death:

Yes, with respect both to his descendants and his kin, the ways of Providence had been beneficent. Yet even towards the end, as he paused on the crest of Beacon Hill and looked out over the Common like one transfigured, he was too much of a humorist not to discern in those ways a glimmer of irony. But for the outsiders—for Blaisdell and Priscilla—the Chippendales might have stood still and died of dry rot. Yet what had he to reproach himself with? After the Chippendales the deluge. So it might well turn out. For not only had they survived, but were more prosperous and prominent than ever. Were not their delicate consideration for the feelings of others, their scrupulous niceties of judgment—and in combination with these their capacity for volcanic enthusiasm for a principle that might seem to mere outsiders but a trifle—still their priceless virtues? (14–15)

Harrison's rosy summation bears correction in some important particulars, and certainly his rhetorical question about the virtues of the New England conscience surviving in the younger Chippendales admits of examination. Blaisdell and Priscilla Avery mark the opposite poles between which the Chippendales proper arrange themselves. Priscilla is not truly an outsider but merely a misguided rebel who finds home. A Boston blueblood by birth and tradition herself, she opposes her heritage in *The Chippendales* but comes to accept it gradually and finally triumphantly in the person of Henry Chippendale Sumner. She stands for a hard-won reaffirmation and consequent strengthening of the old ideals, most visibly personified in a Sumner; she does not add anything new. By contrast, Blaisdell does: modern ways, business shrewdness of a new kind, boundless drive and energy. But his principles are are as weak as Priscilla's are strong, and his allegiance to the clan is relatively tenuous: clearly, he does not become a Chippendale himself. All the same, once attached to the family he abandons his plans of annihilation and accepts his new situation which he has wished and worked a long time to attain. Succeeding Harrison as the head of the family is his son Chauncey who holds the middle ground between Sumner and Blaisdell in *The Chippendales.*

It is the children of this generation who are the younger Chippendales. The war, which Harrison is spared, makes inroads: Henry's and Priscilla's twin sons die in action. And the changes in social conventions which the war occasions continue into the 1920s: there is not only a looseness of social forms quite exceeding anything prewar but a general attempt to redefine life in terms of a new individual freedom, a theme which connects *The Dark Horse* with *The Bishop's Granddaughter.* Three major figures dominate: young Hugh Blaisdell; Annabel Sumner, Henry's and Priscilla's daughter; and Baxter Chippendale, the posthumous son of old Baxter. There is also the familiar theme of adding new blood to the family, here accomplished through the marriage of Sylvia Chippendale, Chauncey's daughter, to Enoch Paul, the governor of Massachusetts. In a replay of *The Chippendales,* Hugh courts Annabel as his father (but more so Henry Sumner) courted Priscilla, and the outcome of his suit will say much about the amalgamation of the clan's opposite poles. Outside and above them all stands young Baxter, to whom Grant quite deliberately assigns the role of a Greek chorus.

The story of the younger Chippendales begins with Harrison's funeral in chapter 2, appropriately titled "The World Goes On." Hugh's friends Amory Langdon and Percy Selden suggest that Harrison had outlived his time; in an attitude reminiscent of reporter Bliffel's "mossback" in *The Chippendales,* Percy suggests " 'that Harrison Chippendale even in his best days was nothing but a dear old fuddy-duddy' " (19). Hugh has been sufficiently moved by the funeral to find this judgment unfair, and when Percy tries to reduce Harrison to someone who " 'blackballed a man for a club because he left the stopper in the basin after washing his hands' " (20), Hugh energetically counters: " 'It happens that the man who left the stopper in was my father. I heard the story as a boy, and remember my father's roaring over it as a cracking joke. Mad as I was, though, it taught me something. Amory's right. The United States is full today of people ready to let the next person pull out the stopper and clean up after them. People especially who've been used to cleaning up for themselves' " (20). Out of this incident grows Hugh's personal ethical imperative, refined and fortified by the influence of one of his professors at Harvard and summarized in the line from Dante (quoted in Italian in *The Chippendales*): " 'Not by lying on down, or under a coverlet, is fame achieved' " (32). For Hugh sees that he must combine his father's energy with the Chippendales' sensibilities: "A good American he meant to be—and not a fuddy-duddy." But the question is: " 'What constitutes a good American?' " (35). Privileged to see Hugh from the vantage point of Harrison's initial summation of the Chippendale virtues, the reader suspects even this early that Hugh will be likely to find the answer to this fundamental question by probing further the essence of the "fuddy-duddy," of whom Grant says that "how to live correctly remained to the end his deepest concern" (10).

Wishing to marry nineteen-year-old Annabel Sumner, twenty-one-year-old Hugh discovers that she is not ready to marry.[11] She tells him that he has yet to grow, and while they remain friends, they drift apart. Hugh goes to Europe, sees the sights, spends over a year in France and a year and a half in Berlin where he becomes "fond of the German people and sympathetic with their claim for a 'place in the sun' " (37). Yet he joins the fight against Germany after the Germans break "their treaty word and were actually marching through Belgium":

Had war broken out without this violation, he would have said, though English in speech, that it wasn't his affair and "Let the best man win." But to break one's word, spoken or written, with dishonest intent, was against the grain of all he had been taught to reverence, the most flagrant sin a Boston gentleman could commit. Old Harrison Chippendale would have risen in his grave in horror at the enormity. (38)

He sustains a disabling ankle wound as his personal badge of integrity. Clearly a man now, Hugh reaffirms in his "half-antagonistic friendship with Rachel Carver" (43) his goal of becoming a good

American. Resolved to follow it in a practical and energetic way, he returns home.

Back in Boston, Hugh visits Henry Sumner, who resembles "an urban, hence more sophisticated, Ralph Waldo Emerson" (56) and Priscilla Sumner, who pronounces "Idaho," the home state of Annabel's husband Roy Wingate, "as though it were as alien as Patagonia" (62). For Annabel is lacking in "background" (59), despite her birth and education, and her rebellion against the old order so signally represented by her parents makes Priscilla's own youthful doubts and aversions in *The Chippendales* look simple. Had it not been for Hugh's admonition, "Annabel would have gone to the man by whom she was infatuated without binding ceremony of any kind—like any wanton woman" (59–60). But the worst is yet to come. Reluctant though they are, both Sumners are willing to accept Annabel's hurried battlefield marriage in France if it was indeed prompted "by a grand passion" (63), yet there are signs in Annabel's intermittent letters to her parents that this is not so, that the initial infatuation has worn off, and that the marriage seems to be breaking up. This would be critical, for, as Priscilla explains, " 'to tire of one another—if this be the situation—after less than a year, becomes for us sheer vulgarity' " (63). With consummate tact and understanding Hugh attempts to interpret Annabel's beliefs and actions to the disconsolate parents; he, after all, is of Annabel's generation himself, of the generation of change. And the need for comfort is great, for to the Sumners "life might well seem a failure if the ethical impeccability on which they prided themselves were to be dragged in the mire by the daughter who had been as the apple of their eye" (66). Though alive to the "bedrock" (the title of chapter 4) they represent, Hugh himself is a Blaisdell and headed for politics, surely not—as Henry Sumner himself advises Hugh—a realm of ethical impeccability. Informed by Percy Selden that the progressive Rachel Carver is in Boston, Hugh is determined to lock philosophical horns once more and to practice political openness as a neo-Puritan Rastignac at the same time.[12]

Rachel quickly introduces him to her neighbor, the Republican kingmaker Virgil Thomas, whose lecture on the political process is an eye-opener for Hugh. An intelligent, well-read, and generally amiable man, Thomas prides himself on his ability to spot and groom likely candidates, to control the political machinery, and to anticipate the issues of the day. Control and timing are everything; he hates "a dark horse" (78). He is very practical and knows that "the well-mannered regular fellow with no special talent" (83) has the best chances of being elected. If this is incidentally a somewhat disheartening assessment of himself, Hugh accepts it as he must, for Virgil Thomas has taken a liking to him and promises political advancement if Hugh behaves himself. At this point, the man ready to come to the fore is Thomas's protégé Enoch Paul, an eminently "safe" man (89). Thomas even has an answer for Hugh's question " 'why it is that the rest of the country is so confoundedly down on Boston' " (85); his theory reaffirms Hugh's personal experience with Rachel Carver and especially Annabel Sumner:

> "The rest of the country are down on us for not joining in the crusade to scrap the domestic virtues. I've figured out that, out of every twenty novels popular today and cracked up by the critics, nineteen have to do with irregular sex interest intent on justifying itself. Husbands or wives with an urge for somebody else. Single women ready to sow wild oats under a halo in pursuit of personal happiness. . . . And don't charge it to the war, son. The war helped it along, of course, but the underlying cause is the new woman. She wants to be free from this time on to do anything she chooses without having stones thrown at her." (85–86)

From here forward, Hugh's private and political experience of the new woman forms the novel's basic structure.

Not only the midwestern Rachel Carver settles in Boston, Annabel Wingate also returns there. Hugh meets her, for the first time in two years, at a party. Influenced by the ultaprogressive Jane Barnard from New York, author of a book called *False Compulsions,* Annabel explains to Hugh what she finds wrong with the old Boston life the outward trappings of which everyone seems to be enjoying at the party: what is lacking is " 'the right to be happy—without hypocrisy or compromise' " (116). This is why she left Roy Wingate when she decided that " 'he bored me beyond endurance' " (122). Ruefully, Hugh supposes " 'that it's up to a man who wins a girl, even if he's brave as a lion, to possess imagination enough to keep her

from tiring of him' " (123). Annabel does not see that view accepted
in Boston, and because she does not " 'relish the idea of living where
I'm expected to apologize for being happy' " (124), she plans to live
in a more progressive city such as New York.

The new woman makes herself felt in politics. Virgil Thomas
senses the gathering force of the movement and wants to head it
off, directing Enoch Paul to make rhetorical concessions to the
women. One of their leaders, Mrs. Daniel Chambers Marsh, turns
into a formidable force and nearly wrecks Enoch's election to governor. Grant weakens this part of the novel by suggesting that Mrs.
Marsh is primarily motivated by jealousy and ambition, and that
she could have been bought off at the right moment, although the
scene between Mrs. Marsh and Virgil Thomas, during which all
pretenses are dropped, is a masterpiece in structure and style. Mrs.
Marsh's terms are higher now: she demands the highest post available
to a woman, National Committeewoman in Washington, in exchange for her support of Enoch Paul's candidacy for governor against
Percy Selden. But Selden's inheriting a million dollars just then
gives Enoch's cause new fuel which makes Mrs. Marsh's support less
important and her appeasement at this time unnecessary.

Aware that Hugh is still in love with her and that she could
marry him anytime she wanted to, Annabel is divorced but continues
to explore her version of happiness. She does not want to be one of
the Chippendales, who "had doddered meticulously instead of lived"
(166). Visiting Jane Barnard in New York, she meets Alan Courtney, a wealthy, dashing, sportive type who like Jane and herself
wastes no time: "She felt for the first time in her life that here was
a man with whom thought and action were really simultaneous"
(215). It is evident that in this respect Annabel is a direct descendant
of Selma White, who believed in spontaneous brilliancy rather than
meticulous reflection. Annabel falls for Courtney; they expect never
to bore each other because they are so natural, and they are to be
free: if they do tire of each other, they will just walk away. The
only reason why marriage is necessary to Annabel is the general
attitude of society: " 'Forms could be consistent with freedom until
decencies had ceased to clash with instinct' " (255). Her happiness
does not last long. Alan tires of her but does not keep his word of

telling her so, perhaps because he cannot face the pain and admit the failure. He and the woman who now holds his interest are found dead, the victims of Alan's excessive speeding. Hugh immediately goes to New York to comfort the heartbroken Annabel. She is shaken and frightened by the burden of the total liberty she has advocated: momentarily, even the Catholic church seems to offer relief: " 'Not to have to think, just to obey' " (384). Hugh and her parents want her to come home, and she assents: " 'The prodigal's return' " (385).

Once again, Hugh has hopes of winning Annabel. This is not without irony, for shortly before Courtney's accident he makes up his mind to propose to Rachel Carver. Rachel, however, turns him down, albeit gently. In the first place, Rachel senses that she is only number two, and that Hugh has come to her because Annabel seems lost forever; but there are deeper differences: " 'We don't really care for the same things.' " When Hugh protests that this is not so, that she has the wrong view of the Boston aristocracy to which he belongs, that " 'we're the best there is,' " and that " 'the only real difference in our aims is that you want everything to happen right off and I'm not always ready,' " she reiterates that she does not consider Hugh typical of the real American: " 'But to be able to see quickly is the true test of patriotism' " (360). Instead, she turns to Percy Selden, whom she has known to be in love with her, and practically proposes to him as from one "fanatic" (416) to another.

Yet Hugh makes progress. Having pleased Virgil Thomas, he is made speaker of the House and becomes an important force in the attempt to elect Lieutenant Governor Paul Governor. Descended from a suburban farm family, Enoch Paul is now the second man in the Commonwealth and sure—barring a miracle—shortly to become the first. But already his thoughts reach beyond the State House, to Washington. The class he lacks is brought him by his marriage to Sylvia Chippendale, who has not only a name and money but also the social knowledge he needs. A shrewd politician, Enoch is basically a decent man and intelligent enough to learn from his wife that " 'laws change, but social principles do not' " (283). It is Enoch's and Sylvia's double triumph—the election victory and their baby's christening—which gives occasion for the family party at the book's end, and it falls to Baxter Chippendale who, according to Annabel, " 'has the best brain in the family' " (382) and functions as a "Greek chorus" (310), to survey the state and fortunes of the Chippendales once more. They certainly have increased and multiplied: "Both Chauncey and Arthur Chippendale's grandchildren seemed almost legion, notwithstanding the talk of puritan race suicide," and it is only fitting that the baby is named Enoch Chippendale Paul. Annabel, too, has come with her parents: "Clannish of her to come—yet why not? She had to live, poor soul. The only two black sheep of the family, Baxter reflected, herself and himself" (433). As chorus, he shares his conclusions with Hugh, who as a Blaisdell has yet proved to be a true Chippendale himself:

"Looking them over today, I had to acknowledge they're a presentable lot. I was proud of them; and neither of us is prejudiced, for you weren't born a Chippendale and they'd be glad to disown me. Dying out? Doesn't look so if you count up the grandchildren. They're still to the fore on State Street, and continue to pay their bills by the tenth of the month. They can be relied on to speak the truth, not to murder the English language, and to be friendly without slapping people on the back. Their churches may be half empty, unless the preacher is popular, but they hew close to the line just the same, and are liable to last a good while yet in spite of the aliens. A little new blood now and then, such as Sylvia's marrying Enoch. But the new blood gets absorbed. Well, you knew that by heart already." (436)

And with a sweeping personal prophecy, Baxter announces to Hugh that he expects to see him " 'governor some day' " (439) and that Annabel will turn to him after all, because she is a Chippendale and will want her children to be brought up Chippendales too.

Baxter believes " 'that the raw stuff which started with the war' " (437) was a " 'delusion' " (438), and he feels sorry for those who, unlike Annabel, do not have a Hugh to turn to:

"The unleashed, cocksure spirits, youths and maidens, who glorified filth in the name of liberty, and rammed it down our throats. The editors and publishers who pandered to the belief that their prodigies had a monopoly of truth because it was stark naked. I'm sorry for the whole outfit. I really am. Because they were so besotted with themselves and so contemptuous of decent people. For only think, they're already in the shadow and their public has turned to detective stories and the private lives of bandits. Boston is a pretty stable place to live in, dear old boy." (438)

It would be incorrect though tempting to declare that Grant, through Baxter, answers Hugh's initial query "What constitutes a good American?" by suggesting that he become Harrison Chippendale all over again. For Harrison was passive; he waited to be invited to run for Congress. Hugh is active; he knows with Baxter that " 'it's compromise, not running amuck or forcing one's ideas on others, that makes the world go round' " (341). And as Baxter says, Hugh would be " 'a big improvement on Enoch' " (439), especially if he were to marry Annabel after all and mingle the new blood of the Blaisdells with the fervor and high principles not of a descendant of Chauncey Chippendale's—the middle-of-the-road man's—but of Henry's and Priscilla's. Thus, the circle would be closed and a line established which would, as Grant suggests in the book's motto, be reminiscent of Biblical filiality and strength:

> 'And they went to the entrance of Gedor,
> even unto the east side of the valley, to seek
> pasture for their flocks.
> 'And they found fat pasture and good,
> and the land was wide and quiet and peaceable;
> for they of Ham had dwelt there of old.'

For they of Beacon Hill had dwelt there of old.

Chapter Seven

"Author and Justice and fine foremost Citizen"

After twenty-nine years of service, Grant resigned from his judgeship on 20 November 1922. At seventy years of age, he could no longer combine "the handling of a large Court with active literary pursuits and other avocations."[1] Devoting his time to his family, his clubs, travel, fishing, and golf, he continued to live a full and busy life. He continued to write, publishing *The Bishop's Granddaughter* in 1925, *The Dark Horse* in 1931, and *Fourscore* in 1934. For a time, he was very active in behalf of a federal marriage and divorce law, but more typical of his avocations than the marriage and divorce essays are his collected poems, issued as a Christmas greeting to his family and friends in 1926.

Occasional Verses 1873–1923

Spanning half a century, *Occasional Verses* is a record of Grant's "frolic talent for satire."[2] "Occasional" has a double meaning, for Grant was a prose writer rather than a poet, and most of his poems were written for a special occasion. They include poetry for college festivities, a great many dinner poems, some family verses, several playlets, and a few others. The volume opens with a deeply felt tribute to his wife, lines on the twenty-fifth anniversary of their wedding in 1908, and runs its course from the 1873 "Harvard Class Poem" to "Verses" for the fiftieth anniversary dinner of his class in 1923. Some of these poems have already been discussed (*The Little Tin Gods-on-wheels* and the war poetry), some can be passed over, and some shall be commented on here, for even though few of his poems have much literary merit, they shed light on Grant's more private side.

A companion piece to the *Lampoon* playlets, "The Lambs: A Tragedy" (1882) recounts the hazards of the stock market. After the discomfiture of Phipps, a customer in the firm of Briggs, Brown & Co., and pertinent grave statements by the three choruses of "Bulls," "Bears," and "Shorn Lambs," the broker's janitor sweeps up the torn ticker tape and the dashed hopes of many a would-be millionaire: "Naught in this world is stable save the fruit of honest industry" (66). "Rondeaux of Cities" (1883) is a playful poem on what the men of four major American cities look for in a woman: Boston—"a cultured mind"; New York—"a pot of gold"; Philadelphia—"a pedigree"; Baltimore—"a pretty face."

"To A. G. G." (1888) is a tender poem to his wife and three sons: "Bambino Bob and Baby P, / Are very, very dear to me, / And so is Alexander." It is a tour de force, as all twenty-two lines end in an *e* rhyme. "Verses" for the twenty-fifth anniversary of graduation (1898) is not only a tribute to "fair Harvard" and her motto "Veritas" but also fun at his own expense: "A Probate judge who deals in verse / Suggests a decorated hearse. / There is not in insolvency / An impetus to poetry." A birthday poem to Thomas Wentworth Higginson's earnest spirit is followed by "The Business Man" (1905), a bitter piece on a hack writer who exploits popular genres such as feudal romances, homespun Yankee stories, and the *Ben Hur* line. Perhaps Grant had Lew Wallace in mind: "An author? No, a financier."

"Lines" was delivered before the Burns Memorial Association in 1920 and not only praises Robert Burns and emphasizes Grant's own ancestry ("I'm Scotch by blood,—my name must show it, / Of Highland stock, yes I avow it / With satisfaction") but most of all gives a timely message to Americans:

> Let those who in this mighty land
> Gaze on your features understand
>   What they inherit;
> That humble brains, to win the crown,
> Must struggle up not level down,
>   Must hold to spirit.

In the volume's last poem, "Verses" for the fiftieth anniversary dinner of his class in 1923, read seven months after his resignation from the bench, Grant looks back over a long and rich life:

> What has life taught us? Zest if nothing more
> To chase its *ignis fatuus* while we may,
> To snatch at fame and power, to see them slip,
> Yet cry undaunted, "I have lived to-day."

If these lines seem merely an echo of Edward FitzGerald's *Rubáiyát of Omar Khayyám* (1859), Grant's awareness and acceptance of the special force of his age add another dimension:

> Our fifty years of fact have staggered dreams
> And dulled the razor edge of fantasy.
> To hear the human voice across the world,
> To see the wingèd plane the clouds caress,
> Electric light, the auto, the X-ray,
> Typewriter, submarine and wireless,
> The deadliest war that mortals ever fought,
> The slave set free and woman suffrage won
> All in one life! Where was the counterpart
> In any life of men beneath the sun?

Clearly, the hum of the mighty dynamo speaks a different language to Robert Grant than it did to Henry Adams.[3]

Grant knew that he was a versifier rather than a poet. Whether the poems "smack of the lamp" or were written "in his bath," whether they are undistinguished doggerel or witty satirical sallies, they are primarily of biographical interest and—like his short stories—of no lasting significance for American literature. In his charming preface, Grant claims no honors for them: "I scatter them upon the sea of time without fear that good printer's ink and paper will render them imperishable."

Service and Honors

Busy as a judge and author, Robert Grant was fond of clubs all his life and belonged to a great many of them; in most of them, he found himself in congenial and rather select company. But much of his spare time was also given to service, particularly to his *alma mater*. In 1895, Grant was elected to the Board of Overseers, on which he served longer than any other member but one; he was its president from 1917 to 1921. He was elected president of the Harvard Alumni Association and of the Harvard chapter of Phi Beta Kappa in 1922 and was president of the Harvard Club of Boston 1923–24. He served on Harvard's visiting committees on English and the Law School. He was deeply gratified when Harvard awarded him an honorary Litt.D. in 1922.

Outside Harvard, Grant's service was also sought and recognized. He was a trustee of the Wentworth Institute, became president of the Boston Authors' Club in 1913, and in 1915 was elected a resident member of the Massachusetts Historical Society on whose council he served from 1922 to 1924. In 1913 he was made a fellow of the American Academy of Arts and Sciences, and in 1915 a member of the American Academy of Arts and Letters. In 1921, he was president of the National Institute of Arts and Letters and received an honorary doctor of letters from Columbia University.[4]

Grant and the Sacco-Vanzetti Case

All of these duties and activities were pleasant compared to Grant's service on the Advisory Committee to Governor Alvan T. Fuller on the Sacco-Vanzetti case in 1927, and none of the honors and recognitions he received equaled the contumely he incurred as one of the three men who upheld the death verdict against Sacco and Vanzetti. The case itself is so well known that Grant's brief summary in *Fourscore* is all the background necessary for the present discussion:

On April 15, 1920, a paymaster and his guard had been held up, robbed, and murdered at South Braintree, Massachusetts. Following the verdict by which Nicola Sacco and Bartolomeo Vanzetti had been found guilty of their murder, counsel had made seven motions for a new trial in the Superior Court and two appeals to the Supreme Judicial Court. All of these proceedings had been denied and the two Italians were under sentence of death.[5]

It is not clear why Fuller appointed a review committee. Many writers cite the national and international publicity the case received, but Cleveland Amory insists that the proper Bostonians themselves were the group who urged the governor to set up the committee: "Having been prodded by one Boston institution, Bishop Lawrence, he promptly appointed another, in the person of Harvard's Lawrence Lowell, to his board. The other two men on Fuller's board of three were also eminently satisfactory to Boston Society—Robert T. [*sic*] Grant, a blue-blood judge of the probate court," and Samuel W. Stratton, president of M.I.T.[6]

The Committee's findings would determine the fate of Sacco and Vanzetti, for—as Grant writes—"The Governor had power, with the advice and consent of his Council, to pardon them or commute their sentence, but none to grant a new trial." Several motions for a new trial had been made, partly on the grounds of new evidence, partly on the contention that the two defendants had not received a fair trial. Given all the publicity, especially in 1927, one wonders whether a new trial could have been fair or whether an impartial jury could have been selected. Grant writes that he was not enthusiastic about serving on the committee but consented to do so "as the matter was one of public service." His nomination "was challenged on the score of prejudice," the prejudice consisting in his strong objection to the timing of Felix Frankfurter's article in behalf of the defendants in the *Atlantic Monthly*.[7] Grant was angry because Frankfurter, a professor in the Harvard Law School, had broken into print while the case was still being reviewed in court. When Grant suggested to Fuller that he be replaced, the governor declined to do so.

Even while the Advisory Committee was at work, Grant was singled out by Vanzetti as "against us to death as he has always been since our arrest and without knowing the case. We know now positively that all he wants is to execute us." In a letter written the following day, Vanzetti likens Grant to Webster Thayer, the demonstrably unfair judge in the trial.[8] Vanzetti seems to echo the opinions of men like Eugene Lyons, who was a member of the Sacco-Vanzetti defense committee and who soon after the executions published *The Life and Death of Sacco and Vanzetti*. Lyons's chapter 21,

"Hangmen in Frock Coats: The Report of the Advisory Commission," is vitriolic on Grant, primarily because of xenophobic statements in some of his books, and sees him as the villain: "Although Lowell was chairman of the commission, Grant's name is the first signed to the report. On the warrant of his title of judge, and because at his age he has ample time on his hands, it is a safe guess that Grant wrote the report to which Lowell and President Stratton of the Massachusetts Institute of Technology added their signatures."[9] Herbert B. Ehrmann, one of the defense lawyers, also held a very negative opinion: "Judge Grant was altogether unsatisfactory. Not only did we feel that he had a black-tie class concept of life around him, but it was reported to us that he had expressed himself violently against Sacco and Vanzetti to some congenial spirits in his club."[10]

In addition to discussing the circumstances of his appointment to the committee, Grant describes in *Fourscore* how the committee worked; he also responds to the charge that the members were not aware of the moral and humanitarian dimensions of the situation. He makes clear that Lowell was not formally chairman of the committee but was so considered because he "was the most eminent man" and acted like chairman. It was Lowell, not Grant as Lyons guessed, who prepared the draft of the final report. Grant leaves no doubt in his chapter as to the committee's unanimity, his anger at the influence of Frankfurter's "specious brief for the defendants," and his contempt for the protesting intelligentsia whose opinion had presumably been formed exclusively by their reading of Frankfurter's article. As to the accusation that the three members showed "a lack of moral and intellectual sympathy that blinded us to essential justice," Grant insists that it is inconceivable "that we men, belonging to a conscientious generation" were "spiritually impervious to justice."

Addressing themselves to that phrase, G. Louis Joughin and Edmund M. Morgan wrote in 1948 that such a charge should indeed not be made against the Advisory Committee, but that Grant "must also be reminded that a just and charitable spirit does not guarantee social perspicacity—or write a report free from grave error."[11] Joughin and Morgan mention that it is *Fourscore* "which gives most of the available information about the Advisory Committee" and declare that "despite his generally harmless nature, Grant was not a good choice. He was defectively innocent of any realistic knowledge of the world in which he lived and he had no important reputation as a legal scholar." They also characterize him as "elderly but by no means senile. A man of modest wealth, traveled, well read, the author of numerous pleasantly innocuous novels." That Grant "was defectively innocent of any realistic knowledge of the world in which he lived" would be hard to sustain; as probate judge he could not help acquiring such knowledge. That he was elderly not only his age indicated (he was seventy-five at the time) but also the frequent notation in the record of the committee's hearings that he could not understand testimony and had to have it repeated.

Yet Joughin's and Morgan's characterization of Grant is both fair and accurate in comparison to some more recent views, the most extravagant of which is Roberta Strauss Feuerlicht's; she focuses on Lowell rather than Robert A. [*sic*] Grant and states: "Lowell, Stratton, and Grant represented the outermost limits of Brahmin Boston; the life of an Italian anarchist was as foreign to them as life on Mars. Though they had not yet been chosen when Vanzetti wrote the phrase, they fitted to perfection his description of 'Massachusetts' black gowned, puritanic, cold-blooded murderers.' "[12] At the other end of the scale, Robert H. Montgomery takes Grant's formalistic viewpoint in arguing that "the Frankfurter book is unreliable in its statements of fact and its conclusions of law" and that it was "a breach of Canon 20 of the Canons of Professional Ethics for a lawyer, whether connected with the case or not, to publish such an article."[13] Montgomery concludes that Sacco and Vanzetti were guilty and had a fair trial.

Some of the charges that Grant was biased against Sacco and Vanzetti stemmed from negative remarks in some of his writings about foreigners of other than Anglo-Saxon extraction. Such remarks occur prominently in *The Art of Living* and *The Convictions of a Grandfather,* but there are others elsewhere.[14] He identified with Thomas Bailey Aldrich's fear of uncontrolled immigration and saw to it as a judge that aliens did not appropriate established American names.[15] Explaining that he had no animosity toward Italians as such but only against the Italian thieves who robbed him twice in 1908, Grant goes out of his way to commend the change he discovered in 1932—only to commit what is from today's vantage point an egregious blunder: "A new force, impersonated by the intrepid Mussolini, seemed to have restored the moral stamina and reinvigorated the enterprise of a great nation."[16] Grant's short story "By Hook or Crook" tastelessly details the discomfiture of the "spaghetti-eating" baritone Spazzopalli who is described as one of the plundering and sneering foreigners who "have no interest in the institutions of this country."[17] Grant also disliked the Irish "pick-and-shovel" men and insisted at the very outset in *Fourscore* that his line was not Irish despite its many Patricks.[18] On the other hand, Grant liked and respected his dancing teacher Lorenzo Papanti; he liked John Boyle O'Reilly, one of his collaborators on *The King's Men,* and he was fond of William Cardinal O'Connell, his next-door neighbor on Bay State Road. Yet none of these three men belonged to the social class represented by Sacco and Vanzetti.[19]

Grant was enough of a law-and-order man to be frightened by abrupt and violent attempts at changing social structures. Thus, he writes to Barrett Wendell on the matter of the Boston police strike in 1919: "We are living in feverish times, but when the policemen struck, the F. of L. bit off more than it could chew. At last the public has waked up to the realization that one class is not the whole community, & shown its teeth. Curtis & Coolidge have been splendid."[20] Harold Laski wrote to Justice Holmes in June 1927, generally pleased about the makeup of the Advisory Committee: "Lowell, I imagine, would be fair; and I think you have some confidence in Judge Grant though I remember that at the time of the Harvard inquisition into me he tended to look upon radicals as noxious insects. The other man I do not know even by name." Holmes had written to Laski in April, telling him that Frankfurter's book had divided Beacon Street and that "Bob Grant (ex-probate judge and author) called yesterday and gave me a moderate statement tending rather the other way"—that is, tending against Sacco-Vanzetti.[21]

Holmes's remark about Grant's moderation seems corroborated by other pertinent information. For despite his objections to low-class immigrants, Grant can hardly be considered an archconservative. He advocated a progressive inheritance tax and favored better workman's compensation and old-age pensions.[22] He was considered a fair judge by lawyers and judges alike.[23] He was able to counter Owen Wister's remark that he, Grant, would never sit down at the same table with Booker T. Washington by a simple "I have."[24] Writing from the editorial offices of the *New Republic,* Herbert Croly in 1914 solicited—apparently unsuccessfully—articles by Grant for his progressive journal.[25] Above all, at least some of his friends seem to have felt that he would find in favor of Sacco and Vanzetti, as indeed the makeup of the committee was widely applauded—even by Gardner Jackson of the Sacco-Vanzetti defense committee.[26] Mark Antony DeWolfe Howe wrote Grant in June 1927: "The confidence which the Governor reposes in you is shared by all your friends. As one of them let me tell you how much I count on your clearness of vision and fairness of mind to contribute to a right settlement of a vastly perplexing question."[27] Much later, his daughter Helen Howe recalled that Lowell seemed never to doubt the committee's decision whereas Grant "never failed to bring the subject up, and always with an attempt at justification which seemed to Father to be wrung from a man who continued to be deeply troubled by the part he had played in the drama."[28]

Such trouble, however, is not visible in the Sacco-Vanzetti chapter in *Fourscore.* Instead, the chapter is marred by a defensive, almost bellicose tone against the intellectuals who believed Frankfurter and agitated in behalf of the convicted men, and by an obsession with the alleged Communist conspiracy that spread news of the case to foreign countries. How little Grant cared about Sacco and Vanzetti when he wrote the chapter is suggested by the way in which he opens the chapter immediately following; he there describes an English capital trial quite different from the Sacco-Vanzetti trial: "What interested me especially was the despatch with which the proceedings were conducted, the cross-examinations in particular, and I could not perceive that the defendant lost any advantage thereby. The man was convicted, and eventually executed. . . ."[29]

Herbert Ehrmann's insistence that the Sacco-Vanzetti case will never die received fresh support through the fiftieth anniversary testimonials in 1977, and his belief that the murders were not committed by Sacco and Vanzetti but by the Morelli gang of Rhode Island was strengthened by the account of an ex-Mafioso in 1973.[30] It would be more pleasant to be able to celebrate Grant as the man who reversed the carriage or miscarriage of justice in the case of Sacco and Vanzetti than it is to review what he actually did and wrote in connection with the case. Had he not only offered but actually carried out his resignation from the committee, he would not have been pursued "with inexorable historic compensation" as, for instance, in Ben Shahn's mural "The Passion of Sacco and Vanzetti."[31]

Fourscore

1927 was a difficult year for Grant. Almost immediately after the Advisory Committee had turned in its report, he and his wife left for England to spend the rest of the summer with their son Robert in southern England. Soon after their return to Boston, their son Patrick died. Grant decided that the years were catching up with him; though he himself continued in good health and spirits, many of his friends and acquaintances were passing away, and he was frequently called upon to write tributes and memoirs. Among these are pieces on Gamaliel Bradford, William Crowninshield Endicott, Paul Revere Frothingham, Henry Saltonstall Howe, Henry Cabot Lodge, William Caleb Loring, James Ford Rhodes, and Barrett Wendell of whom he wrote, "There is no one outside my family with whom I had closer associations or whom I should miss more."[32]

In March of 1932, Robert and Amy sailed on a Mediterranean cruise which took them to Italy, Greece, and Egypt; they saw the Pyramids, the Sphinx, and the Valley of the Kings. Soon after returning home, Robert began to take stock of his long and eventful life. With the help of carefully kept scrap books and dossiers of letters, he wrote *Fourscore,* the "memories of a lifetime" (396).

Ostensibly written as a personal record at the request of Mrs. Grant, *Fourscore* begins with a detailed description of "our descent from clan Allan" (3): Grant was very proud of his Scottish highland heritage. He was equally proud of his Beacon Hill birth, as the following chapters on his childhood, youth, and college years amply prove. He then ranges leisurely over all of the important aspects and events of his life, adapting his tone to the subject under discussion. He mixes the serious with the light, the private with the public, the unimportant with the important—just as he did in his essay volumes. But the subject matter of the essay books is here expanded beyond matters of particular private and general public interest to include his work as a judge and his work as a writer. Although simple chronological development supplies the book's basic structure, *Fourscore* is not just a mechanical succession of events; it is, in fact, quite carefully composed, with much thought given to the balancing of episodes and to the use of material relating to people outside the family.[33] After four hundred pages of information and reflection about himself, his family, and Boston society, Grant concludes the book on a note of gratitude for a long and happy life.

Despite some rather dragging stretches of genealogy and society chitchat, *Fourscore* is a very readable autobiography, and not just because Grant has a great many interesting things to say but also because, as a practised satirist, he often writes tongue-in-cheek and records a good joke even when the joke is on himself. Thanking Bliss Perry for praising the book, he wrote:

Of course I have been a satirist all my days, but with a playful rather than a saturnine touch, and perhaps the claws of my criticism have been pared by time. At all events I preferred to make this a sunshiny book even at the risk of being regarded as a Yes-yes man. . . . And I did not pass lightly over Frankfürter [*sic*] in spite of a detachment as of "Paradise." But as a whole I preferred to let the dead past bury its dead and refrained from dragging out social skeletons.[34]

Although it is sunshiny, *Fourscore* does not have the fault Cleveland Amory charged against "so much of Boston biography—it is too happy."[35]

Grant's Death

In 1933, Amy Grant inherited approximately $400,000. The Grants had always been fond of traveling, and the inheritance made it easier for them to do so. On 18 October 1936, Amy Grant died. They had been married for over fifty-three years, and Robert Grant could say that their "life together had been so happy that I could not have asked anything more of providence."[36]

Grant continued to live as he had always done: alert, interested in life around him, and attached to his family and friends. As late as 1940 he made a trip to New Orleans, the Western states, and Hawaii. Active until the end, he died on 19 May 1940; he was buried in Mt. Auburn Cemetery in Cambridge, the traditional final resting place of proper Bostonians.

The *New York Times* obituary of the following day emphasized his role in the Sacco-Vanzetti case, did not get his age right, and was inaccurate in other details. The next day, the *Times* printed a statement by the American Academy of Arts and Letters: "We mourn the passing of a great man and a great gentleman." The Massachusetts Historical Society remembered him at the 1941 annual meeting: "In all his ways of looking at things and doing things he incarnated the common sense, the public spirit, and the practical idealism of our old Commonwealth." M. A. DeWolfe Howe wrote the Academy tribute, emphasizing the achievement of *Unleavened Bread* and *The Chippendales* and Grant's "personal integrity" in the Sacco-Vanzetti case; to Howe, Grant "was more a thoughtful, and most agreeable, man of the world than a profound scholar." There was a tribute by the Saturday Club in 1948 and finally a balanced memoir by Edward Wagenknecht in *Dictionary of American Biography*. But perhaps the highest tribute had already been paid by Corinne Roosevelt Robinson, who wrote Grant a poem to acknowledge his Christmas greeting (*Occasional Verses*), a poem which salutes Grant as "Author and Justice and fine foremost Citizen."[37]

Chapter Eight

Retrospect: Sources, Influence, Reputation

Grant wrote no literary criticism; nowhere did he set down an extended statement about his own art or his relation to the major literary movements of his time. There are only occasional remarks about these matters scattered throughout his letters, literary tributes, and *Fourscore,* but taken together with the evidence his novels furnish about his literary practice, these remarks permit at least some tentative conclusions about Grant as writer.

Grant's Sources

Grant's early reading left its mark on his early writing in the form of plentiful use of literary allusion, but he never lost the habit of literary name-dropping or surface analogy: as late as *The Dark Horse* he used great writers—in this case Balzac—in that way. He was essentially a passive reader ("I tried to read everything of importance that came out in English or French in the fields of fiction, poetry, or *belles-lettres*") who used his learning as embellishment. In the widest sense, the source for his writings was his own cultural milieu rather than any particular writer or literary movement. This does not mean that Grant was impervious to the literary atmosphere of his day, but when he remarks that his perceptions had been fostered "in the school of Howells and Henry James," he refers to these writers more as presences one could not help noticing than as mentors and models: "While I, for one, did not lack reverence for the illustrious old order already passing, and devoured with admiration the books of the twin celebrities Howells and Henry James then in vogue, I was too busy and indifferent to bother about any of them unless they came in my way."[1]

Howells. Grant first read Howells during his Harvard years; he recalls reading *Their Wedding Journey* and *A Chance Acquaintance* with "delight."[2] It must have been with some aggravation too, because Grant parodied Howells in *The Harvard Lampoon.* "How to write a novel (?) after the manner of Mr. W*ll**m H*w**ls" shows the same criticism Grant would direct at *The Rise of Silas Lapham* later on: "Take one railroad train, with a Pullman palace car, one St. Lawrence steamboat, or a comfortable, full-rigged ship. Any of them will do, but you must decide on one. Put on board a young man of about thirty years old, supposed to embody a withering satire on the first families of Boston, but bearing the same relative resemblance to them that a brickbat bears to an omnibus." And so on.[3] Grant did not attempt to make Howells's acquaintance between 1872 and 1881 when Howells edited the *Atlantic Monthly* from Boston; he was absorbed in his own work and in establishing literary connections in New York.[4] Perhaps he also did not have the courage to seek out the celebrity he had lampooned.

The Rise of Silas Lapham, unlike the two earlier novels, seemed to Grant not to call for parody but for rebuttal:

I had long felt that the most salient novels on Boston had been written from the outside rather than the in. If this were not exact as to Henry James's *The Bostonians,* it was so as to every other, especially *Silas Lapham,* the most famous. Admirer as I was of that masterly tale, I felt that the sympathies of Howells the artist (but also the aspiring democrat) were all on the side of the newcomers and that his knowledge of the aristocratic Coreys, though they served as an excellent foil, was but skin deep, beginning with the selection of their name.[5]

The Chippendales is Grant's Boston novel written from the inside. Specifically, Grant attempts to show by his own characters that there is more to Boston aristocracy than Howells's Coreys reveal. Several of these characters stand out: Priscilla Avery, who at first rebels against her heritage only to discover that there is nothing quite like it after all; Henry Chippendale Sumner, whose steadfast devotion to the "eternal verities" (60) loses him a fortune but wins him Priscilla; Aunt Georgiana Chippendale, whose crusty sense of tradition is laced with humor. But two characters in particular carry

the burden of proof: Harrison Chippendale and his sister Eleanor
Sumner, the counterparts to Bromfield and Anna Corey.

Head of the family, Harrison is a distinguished, spare, tall man
of urbane manners, excellent convictions, irreproachable habits, and
undemonstrative dress, in short, a complete gentleman. After graduation from Harvard, he travels briefly in Europe and fights in the
Civil War before settling down "to the serious duties consequent
upon bringing up his family, preserving his health, looking after
his property and cultivating his mind" (77). Inspired in his youth
by Emerson, he continues to interest himself in civic affairs, although
he never becomes active beyond writing letters to the editor of the
Transcript. He considers himself open to progressive thought while
holding firm to the belief that "what a Bostonian will not do has
ever been, perhaps, his highest title to distinction" (78–79). His
genealogy and that of his wife are those of the merchant aristocracy,
and Grant cannot forbear to say, with a glance at Howells: "In
Boston it would not be necessary to describe the lineage of either
Mr. or Mrs. Harrison Chippendale. All simon-pure Bostonians know
their genealogies by heart. But we are not all simon-pure Bostonians"
(75). Harrison's delicate patriotic sensibility accommodates his son
Chauncey's successful adjustment to modern ways of doing business
but otherwise balks at change: "The whole trend of society was so
repugnant to his traditions, that he found himself continually in a
state of bewilderment" (141).

Harrison's sister Eleanor is equally refined and equally proud of
her ancestry: "Of course she must, as a Chippendale, live with
dignity, but within her means" (69). Devoted to her children and
the memory of her husband, she lives a quiet life and is not inclined
to champion causes like her son and, to a smaller extent, her brother.
It is to her that Grant reserves the most characteristic statement by
a Chippendale in the whole novel, a statement so steeped in New
England conscience yet so free from personal vanity that he reprints
it with obvious relish in its entirety in *Fourscore*. Eleanor Sumner
is inspecting, with Henry and Priscilla, the new Rembrandt Blaisdell
gave the Art Museum. It is "the portrait of a full-faced Dutch
burgher" (242) in which Mrs. Sumner finds a lack of " 'an ethical
quality.' " When Priscilla demurs—" 'But they were like that' "—

Eleanor replies imperturbably: " 'I admit all that; nor do I deny that the art is consummate—of its kind. They were like that. But,' she added in her gentle voice, 'they ought not to have been' " (243).

In his characterization of the Coreys, Howells emphasizes other matters. Anna Corey seems preoccupied with social decorum, not in a reprehensible or vulgar way but enough to make one wonder about her identity. In her treatment of the Laphams, she is guilty of a breach of true manners herself, though Howells partly remedies the situation by her subsequent contrition. Her husband, the gifted amateur painter Bromfield, who spent ten years in Europe and longs to return to live like a king in Rome, also is preoccupied with nonessentials. Discussing civilization with his son Tom (chapter 9), Bromfield feels his way to questions and remarks about Tom's boss Silas Lapham and concludes his cogitations by the classic "It appears to me that there ought to be a dinner."[6] For the next fifty-odd pages, the idea of a dinner dominates the novel, and Howells places the dinner itself exactly at the midpoint of his book (chapter 14 of 27). The dinner chapter is exquisite, far superior to even the best of Grant's writing, but it takes gross advantage of the Laphams' ignorance of social convention, forcing a too neatly double-edged consideration of "vulgarity" as a social (Lapham) and moral (the Coreys) offense.

Grant avoids such a clash. His Blaisdell is urbane, not boorish, and none of the Chippendales, not even the eccentric Baxter, would ever be guilty of the retributive rudeness, however temporary, of the Coreys. Grant's central chapter (15) has Henry and Priscilla charging and countercharging on the subject of Blaisdell, with the discussion of his standards and Henry's strongest allegations against him occupying the exact center of the book (300–301). Both Grant's and Howells's key scenes are fully functional for their books, but precisely because both pit the issues so clearly and strongly against each other does the more genuinely Bostonian nature of Grant's basic argument become visible. The moral rise and economic ruin of Silas Lapham dominates the second half of Howells's book, whereas the Coreys continue as secondary characters. Henry and Priscilla continue as major characters and in fact increasingly assume the importance Harrison and Eleanor have in the first half of *The*

Chippendales, thereby assuring the survival of the aristocratic values. Priscilla's ultimate joyful acceptance of Henry is, to cite Emerson's "Self-Reliance," the triumph of principles which alone can bring peace; Tom Corey's and Penelope Lapham's marriage, noble and touching and desirable in its own way, does not express similarly high-minded Boston notions—and Tom leaves the aristocratic fold. Ultimately, Howells's aristocrats define civilization in terms of taste; Grant's, in terms of moral standards.

Grant did come to know Howells personally during Howells's last years "and grew increasingly appreciative of his charm, and the inherent gentleness of his nature so entirely consistent with firmness of opinion."[7] On 1 March 1921, the American Academy and the National Institute of Arts and Letters held a public meeting in New York in honor of Howells, who had died the previous year. Grant was one of the main speakers. In his tribute, he praises Howells's "continuous portrait gallery of recognizable Americans" and pays homage to "the chronicler incarnate of our manners and customs, of our intimate thoughts and involuntary class reactions."[8] And Grant makes amends for his own former class reaction toward Howells:

I used to think that in his affection for Silas Lapham Mr. Howells was not wholly fair to the Brahmins, whose "toil not neither do they spin" aloofness served as a foil to the inimitable vitality of his most unique creation. A re-reading of this masterpiece has convinced me that he apportioned his mercies equally notwithstanding a latent sympathy, following another American tradition, with aspiring productiveness however homely, rather than the self-complacent lily of the field. (37)

Because Grant does not blindly idolize Howells but points out Howells's "limitations" (38) and triumphs, his final remark carries authority and sincerity: "Often as the words have been spoken already, let them be said again out of our humility and affection, 'His throne is vacant' " (39).

James. The pattern of rejection followed by acceptance evident in Grant's dealing with the standard-setting presence of Howells is repeated with Henry James. Like Howells, James was parodied by Grant in 1879, in the same *Lampoon* piece. If anything, "The

Art of writing a 'Sketch' in the style of Mr. H**ry J*m*s" is even more unkind:

> In the first place, don't have any plot. Let your characters merely ramble round. Abuse your own country like a pickpocket, and crack up everything English. Get a young man of the same type as Mr. H*w**ls's young man, but let him be rather more of a gentleman. Set him adrift in Europe. Find a young, precocious American girl of very bad social position and represent her as a typical American. Make her act like Sancho all over the Continent. Throw in an Englishman or two, and let them all turn themselves inside out and analyze one another as in the preceding novel. When they have analyzed one another sufficiently, cut them all adrift, and let them go on as before. This is supposed to be very artistic. Never by any chance let any of them marry. If you are at a loss what to do with any characters, kill them. Don't have any dénouement; simply say, "This is the end." The whole should be written in beautiful English.[9]

By 1905, Grant had not made much more headway, as his comments to Charles Eliot Norton show:

> By the way, I have been tackling "The Golden Bowl." I wonder what you think of it. It does not become me to criticize so experienced an artist as Mr. Henry James, but I must say that between his eroticism, his diffuse density of style and his reiteration of (his) stock phrases like "You are splendid," "She is wonderful" "& there you are"! I feel as though I had been chewing saw dust or dead sea fruit. Perhaps my lack of perception is the trouble.[10]

For someone who claimed that his perceptions were fostered in the school of Howells and James, this was trouble indeed. But as in the case of Howells, Grant's antagonism mellowed. If, despite the early ambivalence, the avid reading of Howells had taught Grant objectivity and at least a measure of sympathy with common life and had thus to some extent bound him to realism, his late understanding of James showed itself in his liking for England, in his use of the international theme (both of these already incipient in *Face to Face*), in his psychological penetration of the main character, and in his style, all of them maturely evident in *The Bishop's Granddaughter*. Where Grant had felt the need to make a public retraction in the

Academy tribute to Howells, his change toward James is at once
more private and more public: *The Bishop's Granddaughter* is the
homage of a man who had, finally, come round.

Grant's Influence

In his tribute to Howells, Grant managed to minimize his aversion
to homely democracy; he needed no such effort to express his admiration for Edith Wharton, who was a kindred soul. She commented on his novels, made suggestions, championed *Unleavened
Bread,* solicited his help in her attempt to secure the Nobel Prize
for Henry James and in her wartime relief work. Grant was amazed
at her fertile imagination and owed to her the basic incident of *The
Orchid.*[11]
In his Academy tribute, Grant dates his friendship with Edith
Wharton from just after her marriage in 1885: "Teddy Wharton
was thirteen years her senior, a friend of my boyhood and a college
classmate." Later on Grant was able to follow her career as a writer
very closely, since Scribner was the publisher of both. He was a
relatively frequent guest at the Mount. After she went to Europe
to live there, they carried on a steady correspondence. Grant felt
close to her although he did "not pretend to have been within the
fortunate circle of Mrs. Wharton's greatest friends, who beginning
with Henry James formed a special group." His favorites among her
books were *The Age of Innocence, The House of Mirth,* and *Ethan Frome.*
Freely recognizing "her superior art,"[12] Grant considered her to have
in essential ways followed his own lead, and his final comment on
her work reads like one he might have liked for his own: "She told
her readers all that it was necessary to know without violating the
canons of artistic truth, obedience to which she felt to be a requisite
of great literature, the hue and cry of democracy to the contrary,
notwithstanding."
Edith Wharton's *The Custom of the Country* (1913) does indeed
appear to be indebted to *Unleavened Bread,* but Wharton was too
great and too individual an artist to be more than passingly influenced by Grant.[13] Grant was not a major writer, even between 1900
and 1910 when his "books were at the zenith of their popularity,"[14]
and his direct influence is difficult to measure. Owen Wister may

have modeled one of his characters after Henry Sumner of *The Chip-pendales,* [15] and it is conceivable that Grant's early fashionable novels and his essays found some imitators on the hack writer level. It also seems certain that Sinclair Lewis took note of Grant's Selma White. [16] But the most demonstrable influence of any of Grant's books was exercised by the one perhaps least likely to have done so, by *Fourscore.*

The Late George Apley Grant. John P. Marquand's Pulitzer prize novel *The Late George Apley* was published in January 1937. He intended it "as a savage attack on the old water side of Beacon Street" but realized that Apley "had many admirable sides to his character." Marquand "conceived the idea for its structure after having read several volumes of collected letters of V.I.P.'s in Boston (and elsewhere) throughout which were scattered numerous biographical interpolations prepared by an often unduly sympathetic editor." [17] He apparently thought that he had created a new kind of epistolary parody, but C. Hugh Holman suggests that "it probably owes some substantial debt to W. Somerset Maugham's *Cakes and Ale,* and certainly a part of its basic impulse derives from George Santayana's *The Last Puritan,* which he called 'A Memoir in the Form of a Novel,' whereas Marquand subtitled *Apley* 'A Novel in the Form of a Memoir.' "[18] To continue with titles: Marquand's chapter 24 is titled "A Son at the Front," which is also the title of a novel by Edith Wharton.

Edward Weeks writes that "there were some in the Back Bay who accepted it quite literally as a biography and who appeared at the Boston Museum of Fine Arts on Sunday afternoons asking to be shown the 'Apley bronzes.' " Stephen Birmingham relates that the Fiskes were supposed to have been models for Marquand's book and that a Peter M. O'Reilly of Boston brought suit against the publisher in 1938, an action which led to the prefatory disclaimer in the 1956 edition that "all the incidents and characters in these novels are entirely fictitious, and no reference is intended to any actual person, living or dead."[19] That disclaimer, however, is manifestly incorrect for *The Late George Apley.*

In her fine article "Judge Grant and the Forgotten Chippendales," Abigail Ann Hamblen demonstrates that *The Chippendales* and *The Late George Apley* are similar in a number of ways and that Robert

Grant and George Apley have some important things in common, but she does not claim that Apley (or part of Apley) actually is Grant.[20] That claim, however, can be made and substantiated.

Marquand "began to write *The Late George Apley* in the autumn of 1934"—the year Grant's *Fourscore* appeared.[21] On page 297 of his novel, Marquand writes:

To quote the words of one of the ablest fiction delineators of Boston since the mantle of interpretation descended on him from the shoulders of William Dean Howells—"Everything is certain to swing back." This quotation is taken from a novel dealing with our locale published in 1931, when, as this novelist has said, the cocksure new generation "was beginning to perceive that its vaunted philosophy of utter naturalness at the cost of all formulae was Dead Sea fruit." We may quote further the words of a main character, in themselves both hopeful and prophetic:—

The delineator is Grant, the quotation from *Fourscore*, p. 394, and the novel referred to *The Dark Horse*. The main character is Baxter Chippendale, and the further quotation is his statement from page 438 of *The Dark Horse:* "Everything is certain to swing back" to "Boston is a pretty stable place to live in, dear old boy." However, Marquand omits fourteen lines—indicated by ellipsis—and another five lines—without ellipsis. In fact, he reproduces exactly Grant's quotation from *The Dark Horse* as given in *Fourscore*, p. 395. Marquand did not read *The Dark Horse;* he read about it in *Fourscore*.

He read about many other matters in *Fourscore* and liberally used them—sometimes with small changes in detail—to establish the proper Bostonian character of the Apleys and George's biographer Willing. For Willing, Marquand uses the same expression he uses for the unnamed Robert Grant in the quotation given above; George Apley's son John asks Willing to write his father's biography: "You are now Boston's Dean of Letters, Mr. Willing, and now that the mantle has descended upon you, the earnest request of another dutiful son follows that mantle, if the simile is not too involved" (5–6). Later, there is a reference to Willing's article "Harvard in the Eighties," published in *Harper's Magazine;* Grant mentions his piece "Harvard College in the Seventies," published in *Scribner's Magazine*, in *Fourscore*.[22] Another borrowing is a discussion of trust funds (George's father Thomas was "very sure that George would be a successful guardian of other people's money, but not of his own" [116]); Grant, of course, had written on the subject in *Law and the Family* and reviews it in *Fourscore* (337–39). Yet another situation taken from Grant concerns Apley's uncle William, who in his old age married his nurse without giving any warning to the family (251); *Fourscore* briefly takes up old Baxter Chippendale's secret marriage to his stenographer (263).

The list of parallels is much longer, but it is time to look at direct parallels between George Apley and Robert Grant. Apley occasionally writes letters to his old friend from college, Mike Walker; Grant's "chum until graduation was Grant Walker" (79). As a youngster, Apley sees the same type of play (59–60) Grant describes in *Fourscore* (29–30). Apley's views on World War I and Sacco-Vanzetti echo Grant's; both men like Mussolini (337/229); both take very similar views on Hemingway's *The Sun Also Rises* (329/ 383; they do disagree on Sinclair Lewis). Again, the list could be expanded and the similarities shown in greater detail, but one last example shall suffice. This is how Grant describes dancing class at Lorenzo Papanti's school:

I remember him as a florid, good-looking man, a pattern of deportment, who, long suffering and choleric in contact with insubordination, managed to enforce order merely by a rap on the back of his fiddle. At his familiar dancing-hall on Tremont Row, the girls were apt to be prompt in taking their seats on the side of the hall reserved for them; some of the boys were dilatory, with a tendency to hide in their dressing-room, the condign punishment for which was to be obliged to sit with the girls. This involved crossing the well-waxed floor in front of the mirrors and under the big chandelier amid suppressed titters. (45)

Marquand reproduces the same scene almost verbatim, including "several sharp raps of his bow upon his fiddle" (57) and the boys who hid in the dressing room "and were obliged to walk across the floor from the boys' row to the girls' row amidst subdued tittering" (58). But Marquand/Willing pretends not to quote from the fiction delineator Robert Grant; his source is "George Apley, in his 'Memories of a Boston Boyhood' " (57).

Unlike O'Reilly, the proper Bostonian Robert Grant did not start a lawsuit; why should he have? He sent Marquand a very nice note instead, making a point of Marquand's use of the passage from *The Dark Horse*.[23] Had he realized that Marquand had used only *Fourscore?* Had he recognized himself in Apley? To change Harrison Chippendale's belief slightly: what a Bostonian will not *say* may well be his highest title to distinction.

Grant's Place in American Literature

His Reputation.   Measured by the yardstick of sales and reviews, Grant's contemporaneous reputation fluctuated somewhat but was generally rather high. *The Confessions of a Frivolous Girl* sold well and had two English editions; *Jack Hall* and *Jack in the Bush* still sold forty years after publication; *Unleavened Bread* became a best-seller, "reaching a sale of sixty thousand copies, large for a novel with so unpleasant a heroine"; it too, as well as *The Undercurrent* and *The Chippendales,* had an English edition. Many of Grant's books were widely reviewed, not only in this country but in England also, and some even on the Continent. After publication of *Unleavened Bread,* Grant employed an agent to negotiate terms with Scribner for *The Undercurrent,* and Scribner seems to have been advised by the agent that, if need be, Grant could easily take his work to some other publisher.[24]

Grant seems to be regarded more highly by fellow writers than by academic critics. Edith Wharton is perhaps most generous: "Howells was the first to feel the tragic potentialities of life in the drab American small town; but the incurable moral timidity which again and again checked him on the verge of a masterpiece drew him back even from the logical conclusion of 'A Modern Instance,' and left Robert Grant the first in the field which he was eventually to share with Lewis and Dreiser." Some years earlier, she calls *Unleavened Bread* both a great American novel and a great novel.[25]

By contrast, Blake Nevius—curiously enough in a book on Wharton—dismisses *Unleavened Bread* as "thoroughly second-rate." Vernon Louis Parrington finds that novel one of the "studies that were symptomatic of a generation disturbed by the consciousness of a vulgar plutocracy rising in its midst, and yet ignorant of the nature of the disease." It was Parrington who by his phrase "the genteel tradition"—directed at Aldrich—roused Grant's objection: "But Boston, never genteel, but always polite, if cold at times, has not changed despite the passing of greatness." Ludwig Lewisohn uses the proper nomenclature but no more flattering description when he mentions Grant as one of the "polite writers" who "produced stories and novels that had all the superficial marks of good literature."[26]

Warner Berthoff finds Grant's novels seriously deficient: "Painstaking in their representation of contemporary manners and morals, the problem novels of this proper-Boston judge (1852–1940) are without a trace of developed moral perception." In fact, for Berthoff Grant is hardly a literary figure at all: "Robert Grant is chiefly remembered now for the acquiescent though undoubtedly conscientious role he played in the Sacco-Vanzetti case as a member of the Governor's committee." James W. Tuttleton excludes Grant and numerous other writers from his study of the American novel of manners on "the principle that their work does not add anything—materially and in terms of literary quality—to the general argument I have proposed." Gordon Milne discusses Grant as one of the "Turn-of-the-Century Figures," briefly looks at *The Chippendales, Unleavened Bread,* and *The Undercurrent,* and decides that "on the whole" Grant "underplays the study of manners aspect of his fiction."[27]

His Contribution to American Literature. Many of Grant's works go beyond Brahmin Boston and show great interest in the major social problems of his day; he was generally open-minded and progressive in his views. His most enduring creation, Selma White, is a character from outside his own polite way of life. In most of his serious novels, he discards polite writing for a forceful realistic style; Edith Wharton's comment on *Unleavened Bread* details the merits of that style: "There is, of course, no recipe for writing a good novel, and each 'method' is worth just what the writer can make out of it; but I am so great a believer in the objective attitude that I have specially enjoyed the successful use you have made of it; your consistent abstinence from comment, explanation and partisanship, and your confidence in the reader's ability to draw his own conclusions."[28] Grant is rarely this successful in his other novels; partisanship usually intrudes and turns objectivity to satire or bald authorial speechmaking. That Grant does not believe in naturalism almost goes without saying; he stays away from the milieu, and when he does come near it—as with De Vito in *Face to Face* and Loretta in *The Undercurrent*—he does not know how to handle it and lapses into melodrama.

His shortcomings are not his themes—they tend to be timely and important—but his character delineation and his attitude toward change in life-styles and literary modes. The first of these he readily acknowledges as a weakness; the second—his unwillingness to follow change he does not believe in—seems to him rather a virtue, even though it stunted his development as a writer. Grant discusses his failure to create convincing characters quite openly in connection with *The Undercurrent*: "But in making my characters laboriously representative, I lost sight of the quality of differentiation."[29] A few pages later, he repeats what was wrong with *The Undercurrent* (and, one must add, with most of his fiction): "My absorption in a given problem had lured me into making my characters veracious types rather than compelling individuals."[30]

Grant's Brahmin attitude was always with him, but it hardened after World War I: "As I look back I can see it was inevitable that my imagination should have faltered when completely out of step with the new philosophy of life." He was unable to adjust: "The real difficulty was that never having written a word at the instance of literary fashion, I could not bring myself to imitate the prevalent trend." The consequences were grave; Grant "was rendered artistically inarticulate during several years following 1919 by lack of sympathy with much of the philosophy and the grosser forms of naturalism. . . ."[31] The process was visible to him as early as 1906: "I have been told that I am a democrat by intellect but an aristocrat at heart, &, as I grow older, I know this is true."[32] His work had begun—both in subject matter and style—in often satiric imitation of prevailing polite modes of writing about manners and morals; it reached its highest level between 1900 and 1909 when it moved toward the mainstream of realism; and it returned to its original grounds from 1910 on, though with greater seriousness of purpose than his early phase had shown.

Summary. What, then, is Grant's contribution to American literature; what is his place in American literary history? In a 1937 radio address for the Massachusetts Library Association, he referred to himself as an "amiable satirist" and reviewed his career as an author:

> As I look back I can see that my impersonations were sardonic rather than vehement, coarse or dictatorial as many of the American novels most in favor are today. I can look back dispassionately because after 35 or more years many of mine are out of print. I wrote for and of my own generation; mainly about the class I knew best, the fairly well to do, their manners and customs. . . . As a whole my books are a philosophic transcript of social life in the eastern area of the country among the privileged and thoughtful during the years of my activity, and the interpretation of their problems.[33]

In general, Grant's contribution to the American novel of manners is very nicely summarized in these remarks. Specifically, he contributed to the understanding of the workings of fashionable society and to the discussion of a number of important social problems. Fred Lewis Pattee's remarks may stand as a balanced comment on Grant's early work: "Robert Grant's humorous and sprightly studies of society and life were also at various times much discussed, but all of them are seen now to have been written for their own generation alone.—With every decade almost there comes a newness that for a time is supposed to put into eclipse even the fixed stars. A quarter of a century, however, tells the story." For Grant's major novels, a brief recourse to Thorstein Veblen's theory of the leisure class may furnish the appropriate perspective. Veblen details the workings of money and power and describes with great insight the leisure class's "conspicuous" irresponsibility.[34] Grant is more positive or, to highlight his personal and philosophical association with Theodore Roosevelt, more progressive. In his major novels from *A Romantic Young Lady* on and in his essays, Grant is not content to lament conspicuous consumption and criticize conspicuous culture but posits conspicuous civilization and demands conspicuous responsibility. These goals are to be achieved in a framework of manners defined by the most powerful forces on earth: money and love. If Grant's approach is naive, it is nonetheless completely and beautifully American in its refusal to abandon hope.

In their *Guide to American Literature and its Backgrounds since 1890,* Howard Mumford Jones and Richard M. Ludwig characterize Robert Grant's place in American literature well when they list his works as important for the study of "the doctrine of culture in the Genteel Tradition," the development of "the cause of realism," and the growth of the autobiography in the twentieth century.[35] They make no mention of his poetry and his short stories, both of which are indeed his most ephemeral work. Their key term for Grant is "representative": not in the lofty sense of Emerson's *Representative Men* but in the solid sense of the worker in the vineyard. Robert Grant is not a major writer, but most of his work is representative in a very useful sense, and his best work is—to repeat Edith Wharton's phrase—"great American." Certainly *Unleavened Bread* and *The Chippendales,* but also *Fourscore,* a volume of the Fred-and Josephine essays, *The Bishop's Granddaughter,* and even *Face to Face* and *The Confessions of a Frivolous Girl* are well worth reading today.

Notes and References

Chapter One

1. Cleveland Amory, *The Proper Bostonians* (New York, 1947), calls his first chapter "The Hub" and relies heavily on Oliver Wendell Holmes, *The Autocrat of the Breakfast-Table* (Boston, 1858) for his definition of the "proper" Bostonians. In chapter 6 of *The Autocrat* occurs the famous remark that "Boston State-House is the hub of the solar system."

2. See "Boston," in *The American Cyclopaedia,* vol. 3 (New York: Appleton, 1883), pp. 116–28.

3. Robert Shackleton, *The Book of Boston* (Philadelphia, 1930), pp. 42, 20.

4. The "good manners" characterization is "an unbiassed Western view" in James Ford Rhodes to Grant, 3 March 1912. The New England conscience figures prominently in Grant's novel *The Chippendales* (1909), discussed in chapter 5 of this study.

5. The Philadelphia/Boston quotation is from Amory, p. 12. See also his chapter 3, "Grandfather on the Brain." The present chapter is essentially a condensation of the first six chapters of *Fourscore: An Autobiography* (Boston, 1934).

6. For the merchant prince, see Amory's chapter 2, "The 'First' Families."

7. For a discussion of Harvard social clubs, see Amory's chapter 13, "Harvard and Its Clubs." If Patrick Grant knew the waltz, he must not have introduced it in Boston society. According to Amory, p. 262, Mrs. Harrison Gray Otis and Count Lorenzo Papanti danced "the first waltz ever seen in Boston" in 1834.

8. *The Book of Boston,* pp. 321–25. Stuart painted Robert Grant's grandfather Patrick once and his grandmother Anna Powell Mason Grant twice. Robert's Christmas Eve recollections center on a plum cake (*Fourscore,* pp. 67–68). According to a remark by Margaret Homer Shurcliff in *Lively Days,* the lighting of the candles began in 1893 (given in Carl Seaburg, *Boston Observed* [Boston: Beacon Press, 1971], p. 263).

9. Marian Lawrence Peabody, *To Be Young Was Very Heaven* (Boston: Houghton Mifflin, 1967); the title is from Wordsworth's *The Prelude.*

Chapter Two

1. *Fourscore,* p. 69. Further page references to *Fourscore* in this section are given in the text.

2. Letter to Longfellow, 18 November 1874. Longfellow seems to have taken some interest in Grant; by letter of 29 May 1880, for instance, he congratulated Grant on his first novel, *The Confessions of A Frivolous Girl.*

3. "The Little Tin Gods-on-wheels or, Society in our Modern Athens." A Trilogy After the Manner of the Greek. I. The Wallflowers. A Tragedy After the Manner of the Greek (*Harvard Lampoon,* 19 January 1878). II. The Little Tin Gods-on-wheels. A Sequel to "The Wallflowers." A Tragedy After the Manner of the Greek (1 February 1878). III. The Chaperons. A Supplement to "The Wallflowers" and "The Little Tin Gods-on-wheels." A Tragedy After the Manner of the Greek (26 April 1878). "Oxygen! A Mount Desert Pastoral." A trifle offered by Lampy without comment, as an example of the effect that a bracing atmosphere can produce upon conservative natures (18 October 1878). Grant reprinted these pieces in *Occasional Verses 1873–1923* (Boston, 1926), pp. 11–41, which is the edition used here.

4. See *Fourscore,* pp. 116–23. E. C. Stedman and E. M. Hutchinson, *A Library of American Literature,* vol. 11 (New York: Charles L. Webster, 1891), pp. 90–95 print "One Girl of the Period" (from *The Knave of Hearts,* 1886) as a representative selection rather than a chapter from the more serious *Face to Face* of the same year.

5. Alice is a New Yorker. Although there are several references in the novel to Boston girls who would supposedly do things somewhat differently, Grant writes that in his own experience "the differences between the social life of young people in Boston and New York were slight in 1880" (*Fourscore,* p. 123). They were no longer slight by the time of *The Dark Horse* (1931).

6. Richardson, Rousseau, and De Quincey come readily to mind. Grant's title points to the sentimental and the picaresque traditions, both of which continue to flourish in the twentieth century, either in high (e.g., Thomas Mann, *Confessions of Felix Krull, Confidence Man*) or popular literature.

7. From a review of the novel, given in *Fourscore,* p. 121.

8. James's influence on Grant is discussed in chapter 8 of this book. Grant thought that James might have been in some way connected with a sarcastic review of *Confessions* (*Fourscore,* p. 121). See De Forest, *Honest*

John Vane (1875) and *Playing the Mischief* (1875); Henry Adams, *Democracy* (1880).

9. *Fourscore,* pp. 114, 111–12.

10. *Fourscore,* pp. 126, 155–56. *An Average Man* (Boston, 1884) was published as a serial in 1883.

11. Like most of Grant's work before *Unleavened Bread* (1900), this novel has received little scholarly attention. G. A. Dunlap, *The City in the American Novel* (Philadelphia, 1934) uses it peripherally to comment on religious and political conditions in New York during the Gilded Age. In a letter of 28 October 1926 to Gamaliel Bradford, Grant writes that his youth "was nourished on Darwin, Huxley & Herbert Spencer," nourishment which is very evident in *An Average Man.*

12. Robert Grant, John Boyle O'Reilly, J. S. of Dale (F. J. Stimson), and John T. Wheelwright, *The King's Men: A Tale of To-morrow* (New York: Scribner, 1884). One date at Dartmoor is approximately 1967, another—that of a letter from there—is 198?.

13. *Fourscore,* p. 168. For a brief modern comment on O'Reilly and the novel, see Arthur Mann, *Yankee Reformers in the Urban Age* (Cambridge: Belknap Press of Harvard University Press, 1954), pp. 27–34.

14. *The Knave of Hearts: A Fairy Story* (Boston, 1886).

15. On the authorship of "Alknomook," see G. Thomas Tanselle, *Royall Tyler* (Cambridge: Harvard University Press, 1967), pp. 58–59.

16. Boston, 1886. The novel is divided into three books: I. Innocence; II. Sophistication; III. (Un)Common Sense.

17. Grant's reading—particularly for the Ph.D.—familiarized him with the British and continental masterpieces. He was "steeped" in Balzac (*Fourscore,* p. 220). That he knew eighteenth-century comedy is evident by his use of Tyler's *The Contrast* in *The Knave of Hearts.* Tyler's model was Sheridan's *The School for Scandal* (1777), which in turn is of the same type as Marivaux's plays, the most famous of which is *Le jeu de l'amour et du hasard* (1730).

18. Part of the title of Samuel Richardson's epistolary novel *Clarissa* (1748) reads: "Or the History of a Young Lady." For De Forest's concept, see my book *The Worthy Gentleman of Democracy: John William De Forest and the American Dream* (Heidelberg: Carl Winter, 1971).

19. *Face to Face* (New York, 1886). The edition used here appeared under Grant's name (New York: International Association of Newspapers and Authors, 1901). The quotation is from *Fourscore,* p. 169.

20. These two quotations are from *Fourscore,* p. 169; the following one is from p. 170.

21. *Mrs. Harold Stagg: A Novel* (New York, 1890).

22. In its negative import, this characterization of a democratic school-ma'am fits Selma White of *Unleavened Bread* (1900) of whom Grant said that she "was already formulated in my mind" some time before he made use of her (*Fourscore*, p. 220).

23. *The Carletons: A Novel* (New York, 1891).

24. A further indication that Grant sees the representative American family as upper middle class is his use of the name Highlands, which is also the name of the wealthy Mr. Brock's estate in *Face to Face*.

Chapter Three

1. See *Fourscore*, chapter 9, for details on Grant's circumstances at that time.

2. Boston: Jordan, Marsh and Company. See *Fourscore*, pp. 176–77, for Jordan's offer.

3. *The Education of Henry Adams: An Autobiography* (Boston: Houghton Mifflin, 1918), pp. 41–42. Adams describes it as "a battle of the Latin School against all comers." Grant, of course, was a student at the Latin School himself and emphasizes that "the incidents described were real, and often autobiographical" (*Fourscore*, p. 176). Francis Gilbert Attwood was the chief cartoonist for the *Harvard Lampoon* when Grant was an editor; he also illustrated the separate publication of *The Little Tin Gods-on-wheels*.

4. *The Oldest School in America* (Boston, 1885).

5. *Fourscore*, pp. 134–44, 388–89 (on salmon fishing); p. 213 (on bicycling in 1895); p. 40 (on Mayne Reid).

6. In Leroy M. Yale et al., *Angling* (New York, 1896), pp. 179–218.

7. *The North Shore of Massachusetts* (New York, 1896).

8. The edition of *The Law-Breakers* used here is the Garrett Press reprint of 1969 (vol. 58 in *The American Short Story Series*).

9. *Fourscore*, pp. 209, 266.

10. The edition used here is the Cameo Edition (New York, 1895).

11. New York, 1893.

12. New York, 1895.

13. New York, 1899.

14. Philip Freneau's essay persona Robert Slender (1799–1800) signed himself "O. S. M.," that is, one of the swinish multitude. For Freneau's essays and the early American essay in general see Martin Christadler, *Der amerikanische Essay 1720–1820* (Heidelberg, 1968). Nathaniel Hawthorne, "The Celestial Railroad" (1843), reprinted in *Mosses from an Old Manse* (1846); John William De Forest, *Miss Ravenel's Conversion from Secession to Loyalty* (1867; reprint ed., New York, 1955), pp. 50, 65.

15. New York, 1912. Although *Convictions* appeared significantly later than the other essay volumes discussed in this section, it is included here because in theme, style, and persona it belongs with the earlier Fred-and-Josephine volumes.

16. "Nothing human is alien to me," a famous line from the Roman playwright Terence.

17. Arthur Miller talks "About Distances" in the foreword to his collection of short stories *I Don't Need You Anymore* (New York, 1967). In *Fourscore*, p. 303, Grant prints an emotional anonymous letter he received, addressed to "Fred and Josephine."

18. James Russell Lowell's famous tribute to Holmes in *A Fable for Critics* (1848). Holmes's "Breakfast-Table" books include *The Autocrat of the Breakfast-Table* (1858), *The Professor at the Breakfast-Table* (1860), *The Poet at the Breakfast-Table* (1872), and *Over the Teacups* (1891).

19. Grant reprints a number of reviews in *Fourscore*, esp. pp. 207–8, 301–2.

Chapter Four

1. *Fourscore*, p. 173. Once again, this biographical section relies heavily on Grant's autobiography; page references are given in the text.

2. Robert Shackleton, *The Book of Boston* (Philadelphia, 1930), pp. 202–3.

3. *Fourscore*, pp. 219–20.

4. See his chapter "The Evolution of Selma" in *Fourscore*, and chapter 2, note 22 of this study. The "worry" phrase is from Robert Frost, "The Figure a Poem Makes," preface to *Collected Poems* (1939). *Unleavened Bread* (New York, 1900).

5. See Walt Whitman, *Complete Poetry and Selected Prose* (Riverside Editions A34, Boston: Houghton Mifflin, 1959), esp. p. 463.

6. Throughout Mrs. Earle's account one can hear echoes of Henrik Ibsen's *A Doll House* (1879). There is mention of "the Ibsen School" in *The High Priestess*, p. 10.

7. Lyons's speech contains passages like the following: "What is the hope of the world, I repeat? . . . The plain and sovereign people of our beloved country. Whatever menaces their liberties, whatever detracts from their power and infringes on their prerogatives is a peril to our institutions and a step backward in the science of government" (283).

8. *Fourscore*, p. 220. Typical title character plays by Molière are *Tartuffe or The Impostor* (1664), *The Misanthrope* (1666), and *The Miser* (1668).

9. *Fourscore*, p. 231.

10. Ibid., pp. 223 (Higginson) and 108 (Thackeray).

11. Ibid., p. 224.

12. *The High Priestess*, p. 376. *Madame Bovary* appeared in 1856. Grant writes that "at thirty-five" he had been "steeped" in "Flaubert, Maupassant, and Zola" (*Fourscore*, p. 343).

13. In *The Knave of Hearts*, Grant did not write "A Fairy Story" as the subtitle misleadingly advertises. In *Unleavened Bread*, he makes good use of popular and easily recognized fairy tales. There is a pertinent reflection in Whitman's "A Song for Occupations" (note 5 above), p. 158: "Will the whole come back then? / Can each see signs of the best by a look in the looking-glass? is there nothing greater or more?"

14. Or of fascism. Recognized as a forerunner of *Main Street*, *Unleavened Bread* may also have influenced Sinclair Lewis's *It Can't Happen Here* (1935).

15. *A Story Teller's Story* (1924), note 2.

16. *The High Priestess*, pp. 21 (Spain) and 457 (*Lysistrata*); *The Undercurrent*, p. 277 (Elton). The story of the fisherman's wife has most recently been adapted to our feminist age by the German novelist Günter Grass in *The Flounder* (New York, 1978).

17. *Fourscore*, pp. 222–33. The adaption was by Leo Ditrichstein and Grant himself; first performance was on 26 January 1901. One critic thought it should be called "Soggy Dough" instead of *Unleavened Bread*, but Howells praised it highly in the *North American Review*. As for the novel, Grant was delighted by Harry Thurston Peck's review in *The Bookman;* Peck had expected to tear this work by one of the "entertaining amateurs" to pieces but wrote a rave review instead. Edith Wharton called Robert Grant "the first discoverer of Main Street" in her article "The Great American Novel," *Yale Review* 16, no. 4 (July 1927): 646–56.

18. Grant greatly admired the *Forsyte Saga* which began in 1906 with *The Man of Property* (*Fourscore*, pp. 384–85).

19. *The Letters of Theodore Roosevelt*, ed. E. E. Morison (Cambridge: Harvard University Press, 1951), 4:1027, letter no. 3347, 10 November 1904.

20. *Fourscore*, p. 232; *The Undercurrent* (New York, 1904).

21. Grant's model for Mrs. Wilson the aesthete may have been the famous Mrs. Gardner, for whom he named chapter 15 in *Fourscore* ("Mrs. Gardner and Her Circle"). Lewis Mumford has little patience with art collectors of the Gilded Age and their literary associates (chapter 5, "The Pillage of the Past," in *The Golden Day* [New York, 1926]).

22. *Fourscore*, p. 233.

23. Reference to pertinent items will be made in chapter 5 and especially chapter 6 of this study.

24. (New York, 1955), p. 202.
25. *Letters,* 4: 1139–40, letter no. 3490, 14 March 1905. James D. Hart, *The Oxford Companion to American Literature,* 4th ed. (New York: Oxford University Press, 1965), p. 290, defines "the Four Hundred" as a "term applied to the leaders of fashionable society in the U.S. It is supposed to have referred to the exclusive group invited to an entertainment of Mrs. William Astor in New York City (1892), when Ward McAllister cut her list of guests to 400 because her ballroom would accommodate no more."
26. *The High Priestess* (New York, 1915).
27. Letter of 13 October 1915, from Quincy (Grant papers).
28. *Fourscore,* p. 326.

Chapter Five

1. *Fourscore,* p. 247. Further page references are given in the text of this section, which relies heavily on Grant's chapter 14: "Some Friends and Contemporaries."
2. See Roosevelt's letters in chapter 4 above.
3. *The Orchid* (New York, 1905).
4. *The Art of Living* (1895), p. 344.
5. *Fourscore,* p. 273; the next two quotations are from p. 289. *The Chippendales* (New York, 1909).
6. Grant writes in *Fourscore,* p. 263, that "even the clandestine marriage of the aged Baxter Chippendale to his stenographer, not known until after his death and which dashed the hopes of his heirs, fell short of 'illicit love' so far as I know."
7. *Fourscore,* p. 291. The statue of the Bacchante went to the Metropolitan Museum in New York instead (see entry in scrap book, no. 3, 1931–40, Grant papers).
8. For these and the following parallels, see *Fourscore,* pp. 289–92.
9. For Amy, see *Fourscore,* p. 291. Robert Shackleton writes in *The Book of Boston,* p. 307: "It is pleasant to notice on the stones above the graves the frequency of the name of Priscilla, and the dates show that it was a common name, even before the time when Longfellow made it so famous, thus showing that from early days the history of this sweet young Pilgrim girl fascinated the general imagination; or, as Longfellow himself would have expressed it, that the region was 'full of the name and the fame of the Puritan maiden Priscilla.' " Longfellow told the story in *The Courtship of Miles Standish* (1858).

10. *Heiress of All the Ages* (Minneapolis, 1959), p. 103. As its subtitle "Sex and sentiment in the genteel tradition" suggests, Wasserstrom's essay is very helpful for an understanding of this theme in Grant's work even though Wasserstrom makes no direct reference to Grant.

Chapter Six

1. *Fourscore,* p. 238. The following references are also from *Fourscore;* the biographical material is primarily from chapter 17: "Summers in England."
2. See *Fourscore,* pp. 306–323, 251, and the entire chapter 18: "Glimpses of War-Time."
3. First published between 1914 and 1918, the poems are reprinted in *Occasional Verses 1873–1923* (Boston, 1926), pp. 134–42. That volume is discussed at somewhat greater length in chapter 7 below. "A Message" first appeared in Edith Wharton, ed., *The Book of the Homeless* (New York: Scribner, 1916), pp. 14–15.
4. Boston, 1916.
5. New York, 1919.
6. See *Fourscore,* pp. 197, 343, 360–62; "A Call to a New Crusade," *Good Housekeeping* 73 (September 1921): 42–43, 140–44; "Better Marriage Is Within Reach," *Pictorial Review,* March 1923; "Marriage and Divorce," *Yale Review* 14, no. 2 (January 1925): 223–38.
7. The quotations are from *Fourscore,* pp. 362, 363.
8. Letter from Edith Wharton, 26 March 1925; from Owen Wister, 21 March 1925; from Gamaliel Bradford, 1 March 1925 (Grant papers).
9. From "The Art of Fiction" (1884).
10. The quotation is from *Fourscore,* p. 363.
11. If Annabel is nineteen, Hugh—according to *The Chippendales*—must actually be nearly twenty years older than she.
12. The reference on p. 73 is to the conclusion of Balzac's *Father Goriot* (1834–35); like Rastignac, Hugh has shed his last tear of youth.

Chapter Seven

1. *Fourscore,* p. 352.
2. Three hundred copies of the book were privately printed in December 1926. The following year, Scribner's published a commercial edition. The edition used here is the private one. The quotation is from E. C. Stedman, *Poets of America* (Boston, 1885), p. 443. Gamaliel Bradford detected "a certain Horatian attitude of spirit" in Grant's poems (letter of 1 January 1927). Not included in *Occasional Verses* are two longer poems:

the one on the Latin School (see chapter 3, note 4 above), and *Yankee Doodle* (Boston, 1883). *Yankee Doodle* is a satire on Governor Benjamin Butler and written in the manner of James Russell Lowell's *Biglow Papers* (1848). In 1930, Grant read his poem "The Puritan" at the Massachusetts Bay Colony Tercentenary festivities on Boston Common (*Fourscore,* pp. 385–86).

3. See also Grant's "Notes on the Pan-American Exposition," *Cosmopolitan* 31, no. 5 (September 1901): 451–62. Grant humorously refers to *The Education of Henry Adams* in his "After-Dinner Verses," Phi Beta Kappa Society, Cambridge, June, 1920, when he says of the Adams family: "And one has definitely stated / That he was never educated. / But by this means the clever 'feller' / Became a posthumous best seller, / Which rouses the suspicion that / Henry was talking through his hat" (*Occasional Verses,* p. 150).

4. Very good on club life is M. A. DeWolfe Howe, *A Partial (And Not Impartial) Semi-Centennial History of the Tavern Club 1884–1934* (Boston, 1934). For the facts in this section, see *Fourscore,* pp. 252–62, 322–23, 344–49; scrap book no. 2 (Grant papers); *Proceedings of the Massachusetts Historical Society* 48 (1914–15): 496.

5. Grant discusses the case in chapter 19: "The Sacco-Vanzetti Case," pp. 366–74; no specific page references will be given in the text. The chapter has been used by numerous writers on the subject for the information it details about the workings of the Committee. The following discussion is limited to an assessment of Grant's role as a committee member and of his own and others' comments on that role, including his xenophobia; it does not attempt to review the Sacco-Vanzetti case itself. For the Advisory Committee's work and report, see *The Sacco-Vanzetti Case,* vol. 5 (New York, 1929), pp. 4949–5378z.

6. *The Proper Bostonians* (New York, 1947), p. 321. Lowell was president of Harvard.

7. Frankfurter's article was quickly published in book form: *The Case of Sacco and Vanzetti* (Boston, 1927).

8. Marion Denman Frankfurter and Gardner Jackson, eds., *The Letters of Sacco and Vanzetti,* 1928. Reprint: New York: Octagon Books, 1971, pp. 301–3.

9. Eugene Lyons, *The Life and Death of Sacco and Vanzetti* (New York: International Publishers, 1927), p. 161.

10. Herbert B. Ehrmann, *The Case That Will Not Die* (Boston, 1969), p. 484.

11. G. Louis Joughin and Edmund M. Morgan, *The Legacy of Sacco and Vanzetti* (New York, 1948), pp. 302–6.

12. Roberta Strauss Feuerlicht, *Justice Crucified* (New York: McGraw-Hill, 1977), p. 359. Stratton, incidentally, was not a Boston Brahmin. Two other studies, neither of them reliable on Grant, are Francis Russell, *Tragedy in Dedham* (New York: McGraw-Hill, 1962) and David Felix, *Protest: Sacco-Vanzetti and the Intellectuals* (Bloomington: Indiana University Press, 1965).

13. Robert H. Montgomery, *Sacco-Vanzetti: The Murder and the Myth* (New York: Devin-Adair, 1960), pp. 335–341.

14. "The Conduct of Life," in *The Art of Living* (1895), esp. pp. 329–36; *Convictions* (1912), pp. 268–69.

15. *Fourscore*, pp. 249, 313.

16. Ibid., p. 299.

17. In *The Bachelor's Christmas and Other Stories* (1895), esp. pp. 279, 300.

18. *Fourscore*, pp. 3–4.

19. Ibid., pp. 45–46, 170–72, 258. Samuel Eliot Morison, *One Boy's Boston 1887–1901* (Boston: Houghton Mifflin, 1962), writes in his chapter 10: "Those Alleged Prejudices" that he never heard of anti-Irish or anti-Jewish sentiments in Boston society (pp. 63, 66). Conversely, Oscar Handlin writes in *Boston's Immigrants: A Study in Acculturation* (Cambridge: Belknap Press of Harvard University Press, 1959), p. 227: "After 1880, the Yankees would be swept away by a fresh wave of hatred against the foreigners who seemed to threaten their place in society."

20. Letter to Barrett Wendell, 23 September 1919. "F. of L." is the American Federation of Labor. Curtis was the police commissioner, Coolidge—the future president—governor.

21. Mark De Wolfe Howe, ed., *Holmes-Laski Letters,* vol. 2 (Cambridge: Harvard University Press, 1953), pp. 938, 952.

22. *Fourscore*, p. 259; *Convictions,* chapters 4–5, 9.

23. *Fourscore*, pp. 353–59.

24. Bliss Perry, "Recollections of the Saturday Club," in *The Saturday Club: A Century Completed 1920–1956,* ed. Edward W. Forbes and John H. Finley, Jr. (Boston, 1958), p. 9.

25. Letter of 3 December 1914.

26. Ehrmann, p. 484.

27. Letter of 2 June 1927.

28. *The Gentle Americans 1864–1960* (New York, 1965), p. 303.

29. *Fourscore*, p. 375. The man tried "was charged with having put arsenic into the glass of bromo-seltzer of the murdered man, an innkeeper, with whose wife he was in love."

30. For the Morelli theory, see Herbert B. Ehrmann, *The Untried Case,* 2nd ed. (New York: Vanguard Press, 1960) and Vincent Teresa, with Thomas C. Renner, *My Life in the Mafia* (Garden City, N.Y.: Doubleday, 1973), pp. 44–46.

31. The quotation is from a hate letter Grant gives in *Fourscore,* p. 369. A powerful work, Shahn's mural has been "on the outside east wall of H. B. Crouse Hall" on the Syracuse University campus since 1967: see the *Syracuse University Record* 8, no. 6 (22 September 1977): 1. It shows Grant between Lowell and Stratton at the head of the open caskets.

32. These memoirs were prepared for the American Academy of Arts and Letters, the Massachusetts Historical Society, and the Saturday Club. For Wendell, see *Proceedings of the Massachusetts Historical Society* 54 (1920–21): 198. The biographical information in this section is from *Fourscore,* chapter 20: "Autumn Foliage." *Fourscore* was published in 1934 by the Houghton Mifflin Company, a publisher one of whose specialties was Brahmin autobiography.

33. There is in the Grant papers a three-page list of thirty-five questions and problems relating to the manuscript, possibly for review by Mrs. Grant. Grant is discreet in discussing other people, although he is quite open about his own life.

34. Letter of 18 December 1934.

35. *The Proper Bostonians,* p. 63.

36. The biographical information is from scrap book no. 3 in the Grant papers; Grant's comment on his marriage is from a letter to M. A. DeWolfe Howe of 25 October 1936.

37. *New York Times,* 20 May 1940, p. 17; 21 May 1940, p. 23; *Proceedings of the Massachusetts Historical Society* 66 (1936–41): 570–71; Howe, "Robert Grant," in *Commemorative Tributes of the American Academy of Arts and Letters 1905–1941* (New York, 1942), pp. 407–11; William Phillips, "Robert Grant 1852–1940," in *The Saturday Club: A Century Completed 1920–1956,* pp. 73–80 (Phillips wrote the piece in 1948 and relied heavily on *Fourscore*); Wagenknecht, "Robert Grant, " in *Dictionary of American Biography,* vol. 22, supp. 2 (New York, 1958), pp. 257–58. Robinson's poem is given in *Fourscore,* pp. 365–66.

Chapter Eight

1. The quotations are from *Fourscore,* pp. 198, 384, 184.

2. "Howells the Novelist," in *Academy Notes and Monographs,* no. 34 (New York, 1922), pp. 22–39.

3. "How to Write an American Novel," *Harvard Lampoon* 7, no. 8 (30 May 1879): 92.

4. "William Dean Howells 1837–1920," in *Later Years of the Saturday Club 1870–1920,* ed. M. A. DeWolfe Howe (Boston: Houghton Mifflin, 1927), pp. 69–77; similarly in *Fourscore,* p. 184.

5. *Fourscore,* p. 288.

6. *The Rise of Silas Lapham,* Selected Edition of W. D. Howells, vol. 12 (Bloomington: Indiana University Press, 1971), p. 119.

7. Howe (see note 4 above), p. 77. Howells's letters to Grant from 1919 amply show his charm and gentleness.

8. "Howells the Novelist" (see note 2 above), p. 27.

9. See note 3 above.

10. Letter of 14 July 1905 (Norton papers at Harvard).

11. See her letters to Grant in the Grant papers (Grant gave some letters to Yale University). He mentions her in *Fourscore,* esp. pp. 248, 334, 384. See also R. W. B. Lewis, *Edith Wharton* (New York, 1975), esp. pp. 312–13, 335.

12. This quotation is from *Fourscore,* p. 384; all others are from "Edith Wharton," in *Commemorative Tributes of the American Academy of Arts and Letters 1905–1941* (New York, 1942), pp. 362–70. Grant read the tribute on 10 November 1938; the Academy first printed it in 1939.

13. See Lewis, *Wharton,* p. 148.

14. *Fourscore,* p. 290.

15. Wister to Grant, 25 January and 3 February 1913.

16. See Edith Wharton, "The Great American Novel," *Yale Review* 16, no. 4 (July 1927): 648; and *A Backward Glance* (New York, 1934), pp. 147–48. See also Walter F. Taylor, *The Economic Novel in America* (Chapel Hill, 1942), pp. 87–88. Grant thought highly of *Main Street* and *Babbitt* (*Fourscore,* pp. 260, 342, 383) and sponsored Lewis's election to the National Institute of Arts and Letters: Mark Schorer, *Sinclair Lewis* (New York: McGraw-Hill, 1961), pp. 327, 605.

17. The quotations are from Marquand's preface to *The Late George Apley* in *North of Grand Central: Three Novels of New England* (Boston, 1956), pp. v–xx.

18. C. Hugh Holman, *John P. Marquand* (Minneapolis: University of Minnesota Press, 1965), p. 31.

19. Edward Weeks, introduction to John P. Marquand, *Wickford Point* (New York: Time, 1966, p. xiii; Stephen Birmingham, *The Late John Marquand* (Philadelphia: Lippincott, 1972), pp. 87–90.

20. Hamblen's article appeared in *University of Kansas City Review* 33 (1967): 175–79.

21. Marquand, 1956 preface, p. xvii.

22. *Fourscore,* pp. 76–77.

23. Letter of 4 February 1937.

24. The quotation is from *Fourscore,* p. 224. The other references are from pp. 122, 178, 294, 235; they are representative, not exhaustive.

25. See note 16 above.

26. Nevius, *Edith Wharton* (Berkeley and Los Angeles, University of California Press, 1953), p. 148; Parrington, *Main Currents in American Thought,* vol. 3 (New York, 1930), p. 180; *Fourscore,* p. 250; Lewisohn, *Expression in America* (New York, 1932), p. 94.

27. Berthoff, *The Ferment of Realism* (New York, 1965), pp. 132–33; Tuttleton, *The Novel of Manners in America* (Chapel Hill, 1972), pp. xii–xiii; Milne, *The Sense of Society* (Rutherford, N. J., 1977), pp. 107–14.

28. *Fourscore,* p. 223.

29. Ibid., pp. 232–33. See also p. 78 above.

30. *Fourscore,* p. 237.

31. Ibid., pp. 342, 343–44.

32. Letter of 28 October 1906 to Barrett Wendell.

33. "Radio Address for Massachusetts Library Association—a personal profile," 18 May 1937, p. 7 (scrap book no. 3 in the Grant papers).

34. Fred Lewis Pattee, *A History of American Literature Since 1870* (New York, 1917), p. 409; Thorstein Veblen, *The Theory of the Leisure Class* (Boston, 1973 [1899]).

35. Howard Mumford Jones and Richard M. Ludwig, *Guide to American Literature and its Backgrounds since 1890,* 3d ed. (Cambridge, Mass., 1964), pp. 121, 122, 145, 146, 212.

Selected Bibliography

PRIMARY SOURCES

1. Bibliography

Foley, P.K. *American Authors 1795–1895*. Kennebunkport, Maine: Milford House, 1969, pp. 104–5.

Wright, Lyle H. *American Fiction 1876–1900: A Contribution Toward a Bibliography*. San Marino, Calif.: Huntington Library, 1966, pp. 225–27.

2. Manuscripts

Cambridge. Harvard University. Archives. Robert Grant. "Shakespeare's Sonnets: the various theories that have been given to account for them." Ph.D. dissertation, 1876. Signed and dated "Robert Grant, December, 1875." Forty-eight pages.

———. Harvard University. Houghton Library. Robert Grant papers. Given in memory of Robert Grant, class of 1873, by his sons, Robert Grant Jr., Alexander Galt Grant, and Gordon Grant. Received 22 July 1940. Typewritten 47-page catalog listing 785 entries.

Robbins, J. Albert, ed. *American Literary Manuscripts*. 2d ed. Athens: University of Georgia Press, 1977, p. 130.

3. Published Works

The Art of Living. New York: Charles Scribner's, 1895.

An Average Man. Boston: J. R. Osgood, 1884.

The Bachelor's Christmas and Other Stories. New York: Charles Scribner's, 1895.

The Bishop's Granddaughter. New York: Charles Scribner's, 1925.

The Carletons: A novel. New York: Robert Bonner's, 1891.

The Chippendales. New York: Charles Scribner's, 1909.

The Confessions of a Frivolous Girl: A Story of Fashionable Life. Boston: A. Williams, 1880.

The Convictions of a Grandfather. New York: Charles Scribner's, 1912.

The Dark Horse. A Story of the Younger Chippendales. Boston: Houghton Mifflin, 1931.

"Edith Wharton." In *Commemorative Tributes of the American Academy of Arts and Letters 1905–1941*. New York: American Academy of Arts and Letters, 1942, pp. 362–70. First delivered in 1938.

Face to Face. New York: Charles Scribner's, 1886. Published anonymously.

Fourscore: An Autobiography. Boston: Houghton Mifflin, 1934.

The High Priestess. New York: Charles Scribner's, 1915.

"Howells the Novelist." In *Academy Notes and Monographs*, no. 34. New York: American Academy of Arts and Letters, 1922, pp. 22–39.

Jack Hall; or, The School Days of an American Boy. Boston: Jordan, Marsh, 1887.

Jack in the Bush; or, a Summer on a Salmon River. Boston: Jordan, Marsh, 1888.

The King's Men: A Tale of To-morrow. New York: Charles Scribner's, 1884. With John Boyle O'Reilly, J. S. of Dale (i.e., Frederic J. Stimson), and John T. Wheelwright.

The Knave of Hearts: A Fairy Story. Boston: Ticknor, 1886.

The Lambs: A tragedy. Boston: J. R. Osgood, 1883.

Law and the Family. New York: Charles Scribner's, 1919.

The Law-Breakers, and Other Stories. New York: Charles Scribner's, 1906. Reprint: New York: Garrett Press, 1969 (*The American Short Story Series*, 58).

The Little Tin Gods-on-wheels; or, Society in Our Modern Athens: A trilogy after the manner of the Greek. Cambridge, Mass.: C. W. Sever, 1879. Also includes "Oxygen! A Mt. Desert Pastoral."

Mrs. Harold Stagg: A novel. New York: Robert Bonner's, 1890.

The North Shore of Massachusetts. American Summer Resorts. 1894. Reprint: New York: Charles Scribner's, 1896.

Occasional Verses 1873–1923. Boston: Privately printed [D. B. Updike, Merrymount Press], 1926.

The Oldest School in America. An oration by Phillips Brooks, D.D., and a poem by Robert Grant, at the celebration of the two hundred and fiftieth anniversary of the foundation of the Boston Latin school, April 23, 1885. Boston: Houghton, Mifflin, 1885.

The Opinions of a Philosopher. New York: Charles Scribner's, 1893.

The Orchid. New York: Charles Scribner's, 1905.

The Reflections of a Married Man. New York: Charles Scribner's, 1892.

A Romantic Young Lady. Boston: Ticknor, 1886.

Search-Light Letters. New York: Charles Scribner's, 1899.

"Tarpon Fishing in Florida." In *Angling,* by Leroy Milton Yale et al. Out
of Door Library. New York: Charles Scribner's, 1896, pp. 179–218.
*Their Spirit: Some Impressions of the English and French During the Summer of
1916.* Boston: Houghton Mifflin, 1916.
The Undercurrent. New York: Charles Scribner's, 1904.
Unleavened Bread. New York: Charles Scribner's, 1900.
Yankee Doodle. A poem delivered before the Phi Beta Kappa Society of
Harvard University, June 28, 1883. Boston: Cupples, Upham, 1883.

SECONDARY SOURCES

1. Criticism

Berthoff, Warner. *The Ferment of Realism: American Literature, 1884–1919.*
New York: Free Press, 1965. Brief unsympathetic comment on *Unleavened Bread* and Grant's other problem novels.

Blake, Fay M. *The Strike in the American Novel.* Metuchen, N. J.: Scarecrow
Press, 1972. Brief mention of *Face to Face.*

Brooks, Van Wyck. *New England: Indian Summer 1865–1915.* New York:
E. P. Dutton, 1940. Brief but excellent comment on Grant as Boston
author.

Dunlap, George Arthur. *The City in the American Novel, 1789–1900: A
Study of American Novels Portraying Contemporary Conditions in New York,
Philadelphia, and Boston.* 1934. Reprint: New York: Russell & Russell,
1965. Brief mention of *An Average Man* and *Unleavened Bread* as they
reflect city life.

Eichelberger, Clayton L., comp. *A Guide to Critical Reviews of United States
Fiction, 1870–1910.* 2 vols. Metuchen, N. J.: Scarecrow Press,
1971–74. Important listing of newspaper and magazine reviews of
Grant's books for the time indicated.

Hamblen, Abigail Ann. "Judge Grant and the Forgotten Chippendales."
University of Kansas City Review 33 (1967): 175–79. Demonstrates the
connection between *The Chippendales* and John P. Marquand's *The Late
George Apley.*

Howe, Mark Antony DeWolfe. "Robert Grant." In *Commemorative Tributes
of the American Academy of Arts and Letters 1905–1941.* New York:
Academy of Arts and Letters, 1942, pp. 407–11. Balanced and sympathetic biographical and critical sketch by a friend.

Jones, Howard Mumford, and Ludwig, Richard M. *Guide to American
Literature and its Backgrounds since 1890.* 3d ed. Cambridge: Harvard

University Press, 1964. Mentions Grant's essays, major novels, and autobiography as representative of their time and genre.

Knight, Grant C. *The Strenuous Age in American Literature.* Chapel Hill: University of North Carolina Press, 1954. Hurried comment—based on *Fourscore*—on *Unleavened Bread* and *The Chippendales.*

Lewisohn, Ludwig. *Expression in America.* New York: Harper, 1932. Brief mention of Grant as one of the "polite writers."

Milne, Gordon. *The Sense of Society: A History of the American Novel of Manners.* Rutherford, N. J.: Fairleigh Dickinson University Press, 1977. Limited discussion of Grant as a novelist of manners.

Obojski, Robert Thaddeus. "Robert Grant. Satirist of Old Boston and Intellectual Leader of the New." Ph.D. dissertation, Western Reserve University, 1955. To date, the only thesis on Grant. Solid pioneering study; sometimes more panorama than literary criticism.

Parrington, Vernon Louis. *Main Currents in American Thought.* Vol. 3. *The Beginnings of Critical Realism in America: 1860–1920.* New York: Harcourt, Brace, 1930. Places Grant with Wharton and Boyesen.

Pattee, Fred Lewis. *A History of American Literature Since 1870.* New York: Century, 1917. Brief comment on Grant's "humorous and sprightly studies of society and life."

Quinn, Arthur Hobson. *American Fiction: An Historical and Critical Survey.* New York: Appleton-Century, 1936. Fullest discussion of Grant's work; relies on *Fourscore.*

Stedman, Edmund Clarence. *Poets of America.* Boston: Houghton, Mifflin, 1885. "Robert Grant has a frolic talent for satire, and something like that masterhood of current styles for which we still read Frere and Aytoun."

Taylor, Walter F. *The Economic Novel in America.* Chapel Hill: University of North Carolina Press, 1942. Brief discussion of *Unleavened Bread.*

Wagenknecht, Edward. "Robert Grant." In *Dictionary of American Biography.* Vol. 22, supp. 2. New York: Charles Scribner's, 1958, pp. 257–58. Fine biographical and critical sketch.

Walker, Robert H. *The Poet and the Gilded Age: Social Themes in Late 19th Century American Verse.* Philadelphia: University of Pennsylvania Press, 1963. Brief mention of Grant's poetry.

Wharton, Edith. "The Great American Novel." *Yale Review* 16, no. 4 (July 1927): 646–56. Grant as the discoverer of Main Street.

———. *A Backward Glance.* New York: Appleton-Century, 1934. High praise of *Unleavened Bread* by a distinguished friend and fellow novelist.

2. Background

Allen, Frederick Lewis. *Only Yesterday.* 1931. Reprint: New York: Bantam Books, 1959. America from World War I to the depression.

Amory, Cleveland. *The Proper Bostonians.* New York: E. P. Dutton, 1947. Amusing, critical, and useful study of blue-blood Boston.

Brooks, Van Wyck. *From the Shadow of the Mountain: My Post-Meridian Years.* New York: E. P. Dutton, 1961. Personal recollection of Grant in his old age.

Brown, Herbert Ross. *The Sentimental Novel in America 1789–1860.* Durham, N. C.: Duke University Press, 1940. Discusses a tradition Grant both followed and satirized.

Christadler, Martin. *Der amerikanische Essay 1720–1820.* Beihefte zum Jahrbuch für Amerikastudien, vol. 25. Heidelberg: Carl Winter, 1968. Important for the essay tradition Grant continued.

Ehrmann, Herbert B. *The Case That Will Not Die: Commonwealth vs. Sacco and Vanzetti.* Boston: Little, Brown, 1969. "Judge Grant was altogether unsatisfactory."

Forbes, Edward W. and Finley, John H. Jr., eds. *The Saturday Club: A Century Completed 1920–1956.* Boston: Houghton Mifflin, 1958. Includes material on and by Grant.

Frankfurter, Felix. *The Case of Sacco and Vanzetti: A Critical Analysis for Lawyers and Laymen.* Boston: Little, Brown, 1927. The famous pro–Sacco-Vanzetti piece which angered Grant because of its untimely publication.

Grant, Amy Gordon, comp. *Letters from Armageddon.* Boston: Houghton Mifflin, 1930. A collection of World War I letters made by Grant's wife.

Green, Martin. *The Problem of Boston: Some Readings in Cultural History.* New York: Norton, 1966. Critical view of old Boston.

Hardwick, Elizabeth. "Boston." In *A View of My Own: Essays in Literature and Society.* New York: Farrar, Straus and Cudahy, 1962. A modern love-hate piece on Boston.

Hofstadter, Richard. *The Age of Reform: From Bryan to F. D. R.* New York: Vintage Books, 1955. Celebrated study of the progressive movement with which Grant identifed to some extent.

Howe, Helen. *The Gentle Americans 1864–1960: Biography of a Breed.* New York: Harper & Row, 1965. Brief recollections of Grant.

Howe, Mark Antony DeWolfe. *Boston, The Place and the People.* New York: Macmillan, 1903. Description of Grant's Boston by a friend.

———. *A Partial (And Not Impartial) Semi-Centennial History of the Tavern Club 1884–1934.* Boston: Printed for the Tavern Club, 1934. An excellent account of the kind of club life Grant was fond of, with information about and material by him.

Joughin, G. Louis and Morgan, Edmund M. *The Legacy of Sacco and Vanzetti.* New York: Harcourt, Brace, 1948. Critical of Grant in a responsible way.

Lewis, R. W. B. *Edith Wharton: A Biography.* New York: Harper & Row, 1975. Important for Grant's friendship with Wharton.

Marquand, John P. Preface to *The Late George Apley.* In *North of Grand Central: Three Novels of New England.* Boston: Little, Brown, 1956. Important in the context of Marquand's use of Grant in *The Late George Apley.*

Mumford, Lewis. *The Golden Day: A Study in American Experience and Culture.* New York: Boni and Liveright, 1926. Incisive discussion of the European view taken by leading proper Bostonians of Grant's day.

The Sacco-Vanzetti Case: Transcript of the Record of the Trial of Nicola Sacco and Bartolomeo Vanzetti in the Courts of Massachusetts and Subsequent Proceedings 1920–7. Vol. 5. New York: Henry Holt, 1929. Contains the hearings and report of the Advisory Committee of which Grant was a member.

Shackleton, Robert. *The Book of Boston.* 1916. Reprint: Philadelphia: Penn Publishing, 1930. Detailed description of Grant's Boston.

Tuttleton, James W. *The Novel of Manners in America.* Chapel Hill: University of North Carolina Press, 1972. Important study of the genre; excludes Grant because his work "does not add anything—materially and in terms of literary quality—to the general argument I have proposed."

Veblen, Thorstein. *The Theory of the Leisure Class.* 1899. Reprint: With an Introduction by John Kenneth Galbraith. Boston: Houghton Mifflin, 1973. Famous work against which some of Grant's basic views must be seen.

Warren, Austin. *The New England Conscience.* Ann Arbor: University of Michigan Press, 1966. Discussion of a concept central to Grant's personality and work.

Wasserstrom, William. *Heiress of All the Ages: Sex and Sentiment in the Genteel Tradition.* Minneapolis: University of Minnesota Press, 1959. An essay important for the understanding of Grant's view of woman.

Ziff, Larzer. *The American 1890s: Life and Times of a Lost Generation.* New York: Viking Press, 1966. A study of writers who, unlike Grant, did not stand in the Brahmin tradition.

Index

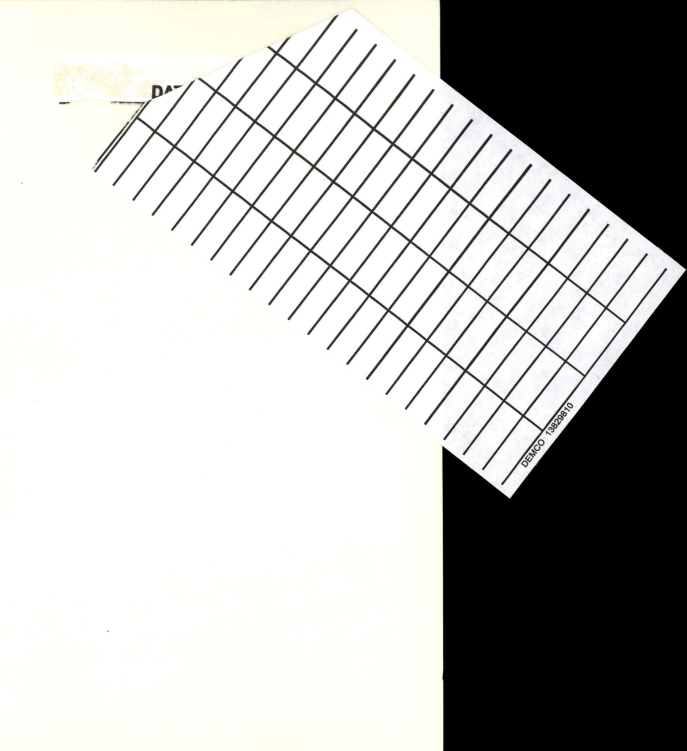